'A strik...ly n... ...ipping back life to its bare essentials to u... ...st... ...wh... ...important. Some beautiful descriptions of nature and survival.'
Vassos Alexander, BBC Radio 2

'Engaging, smart, and full of adventure. This book vividly illustrates the power of running, nature, and the human soul in overcoming obstacles and finding joy.'
Mackenzie Lobby Havey, author of *Mindful Running*

'A fascinating story about a man dedicated and entirely devoted to his true love – running.'
Dean Karnazes, ultra-marathoner and *The New York Times* bestselling author

'A frank, vivid and muscular memoir. His story will stun you and teach you about running, escape and life itself.'
Chas Newkey-Burden, journalist and author

'Celebrates the sheer instinctive naturalness of running.'
Phil Hewitt, bestselling author of *Keep on Running* and *Outrunning the Demons*

'Torgeby has reached the runner's promised land, a place of complete physical freedom. The whole book twitches with his urge to outrun the world, to escape the track and return to the trees. At its best, reading *The Runner* is like following a deer in flight. Torgeby's claustrophobic rage evaporates when he's on the move, his problems fall behind the rhythm of his heart and limbs.'
Jack Cooke, author of *The Tree-Climber's Guide*

'There is nothing superfluous or pointless in this book. Only heart and taut verbal muscle.'
Bodil Juggas, *Arbetabladet*

'Poetic, direct and honest. Read it!'
Maria Kustvik, *Östgöta Correspondenten*

WAL...
D0544073
90

THE
RUNNER

Four Years Living and Running in the Wilderness

MARKUS TORGEBY

BLOOMSBURY SPORT

LONDON · OXFORD · NEW YORK · NEW DELHI · SYDNEY

BLOOMSBURY SPORT
Bloomsbury Publishing Plc
50 Bedford Square, London, WC1B 3DP, UK

BLOOMSBURY, BLOOMSBURY SPORT and the Diana logo are trademarks of
Bloomsbury Publishing Plc

First published in Sweden in 2015 as *Löparens Hjärta* by Offside Press,
by agreement with the Kontext Agency

First published in Great Britain in 2018
This edition published 2019

Copyright © Markus Torgeby, 2018

Markus Torgeby has asserted his right under the Copyright, Designs and
Patents Act, 1988, to be identified as Author of this work

Translated by Karl French

Page 8: private collection; page 58: image by Gabriel Wennstig; page 94: image
by Peter Magnusson/Helion Films; page 124: image by Frida Torgeby;
page 156: private collection; pages 180–181: map courtesy of Offside Press AB.

All Peter Magnusson's pictures are taken from the film *Löparen* (2002).
Read more about the film at helionfilm.se.

All rights reserved. No part of this publication may be reproduced or transmitted
in any form or by any means, electronic or mechanical, including photocopying,
recording, or any information storage or retrieval system, without prior
permission in writing from the publishers

A catalogue record for this book is available from the British Library.

Library of Congress Cataloguing-in-Publication data has been applied for.

ISBN: PB: 978-1-4729-7420-4; eBook: 978-1-4729-5496-1

2 4 6 8 10 9 7 5 3 1

Typeset in Sabon by Deanta Global Publishing Services, Chennai, India
Printed and bound in the UK by CPI Group (UK) Ltd, Croydon, CR0 4YY

MIX
Paper from
responsible sources
FSC® C020471

To find out more about our authors and books visit www.bloomsbury.com
and sign up for our newsletters

For Frida

Waltham Forest Libraries

904 000 00661812

Askews & Holts	12-Nov-2019
796.424 TOR	£9.99
6184108	L

CONTENTS

There will come a time when people are mad, and when they meet someone who isn't mad, they'll turn to him and say, 'You are mad', because he isn't like them.

Antonius, *Apophthegmata Patrum*
[Sayings of the Desert Fathers]

INTRODUCTION

Jämtland, northern Sweden, February 2018 (outside temperature –22°)

I have run every day for the last 25 years. I love running, I love feeling my heart beating in my chest. Just existing in the physical world, when my legs respond and the sweat is pouring down my back.

It's as if my head and my thoughts become clearer as I listen to my heart.

As if I am standing outside myself, looking in.

There is not always much thought, but a sense of being in the moment.

* * *

The book I have written isn't about how to become a faster runner. It is, rather, a book about how you can use your body to open up the door leading into your heart. How you can use running to become a better person.

To become the person you are meant to be.

When I began running seriously many years ago, my only focus was to train in order to run as fast as possible. To win, to be the best. I pictured myself taking part in important races, and I felt I was on track.

Life got in the way, bringing illness, death and grief. Here was a deep well of anxiety, and I found myself right at the bottom of it. My head was full of dark thoughts. I didn't know what to do.

I had to rethink what it was I really wanted, I had to find a way out of that well.

My search brought me into the woods. I lived alone in a Sami yurt in northern Sweden for four years.

I experienced extreme cold, and I felt the joy when the sun brought back the warmth in springtime. I fought the struggles that people have faced through the ages. I encountered problems that our bodies are equipped to cope with – and found solutions we have discarded in the lives we lead now.

I had to go back to basics in order to find my way.

I fed on solitude and nature.

* * *

It's impossible to get away from yourself when you are on your own. I think that leaving everything to move out into the woods seems tempting to a lot of people. To live a life without stress. I find it strange that more people don't do this. Imagine being woken up early one morning in the spring by the sun warming the canvas of your tent. Drinking a little warm water with some honey and getting into your running gear. Running through the woods along the rough tracks made by wild animals. Alone with the smell of fir trees, the sun shining through the branches. The heat builds in your body as you run up the hills.

Pausing, alone, at the top, you are faced with endless vistas stretching in every direction. You breathe deeply.

* * *

The sun has just set.

The shadows from the trees have gone.

No lights as far as the eye can see, the darkness is complete.

I light the birch wood in the burner, feeling the heat on my face. I see the flames flickering through the glass. This is my TV.

The children are asleep in the loft. My wife is down south, working in the other world.

I realise that everything in life is cyclical.

And that as long as I am in the moment all will be well.

Markus Torgeby, 2018

PROLOGUE

Jämtland, northern Sweden, autumn 1999

IT'S THE AFTERNOON The sun is tired, but the light is warm, and I run from the Slagsån up to the marsh below Romohöjden. The snow is sticking on top of Åreskutan. I run across the marsh and my legs feel light.

I run in giant strides across the mountain slopes, all the way down to the Indalsälven and past the Ristafallet. I continue down the path along the river and get back on the hill, three kilometres of steep uphill running. I move effortlessly and come back to the marsh with the sun on my back.

Then I hear the call of an elk. I stop. After a while, I hear another elk answering a bit further away. I put my thumb and index finger across my nose and make a call of my own and both elks answer.

They are both quite close and I stand still. At last they come out onto the marsh with 30 metres between them. I don't move. Nor do the elks, and their big ears are pointing towards me like satellite dishes. We form a triangle – the bull, the cow and I. The elks have got the evening sun in their eyes and the wind at their backs. Their legs are long and thin, and they look strong.

I run on and so do the elks. There are crashing sounds from the forest as they disappear.

When I reach Helgesjön I take off my clothes and jump in, and swim around until the mud and sweat has been washed away. I rub my armpits with sand and walk naked through the forest all the way back home to the tent.

I put on my underclothes, my thick socks and hat. Steam comes from my mouth when I breathe out. I go out into the forest to collect birch bark and fine twigs to use as kindling. I split some logs for when the fire has taken. I build the fire up with bigger and bigger branches. I keep the fire going until it's warm inside the tent, and I warm away the dampness from the canvas.

The forest is silent. My face is warm from the fire. Outside there's a wall of darkness.

I eat crispbread with butter and drink some warm water, let the fire burn down and go to bed. I write down the events of the day in my diary. I watch the stars through the smoke vent.

I like lying there wrapped up in my sleeping bag, feeling the cold night air against my face.

ÖCKERÖ

IT'S CHRISTMAS EVE 1985 and Mum has a headache. The world is spinning, she says. She's having problems with her balance.

I am nine, the eldest of four. My two sisters are one and three years younger than me, and my little brother is two.

We're having Christmas with our cousins who live in a house nearby; you just walk down the hill and there you are. I have made a fishing boat in woodwork for Grandma and Grandad. The boat is called *Kristina* just like Grandad's. They showed it in an exhibition at school, so I'm really happy.

Mum goes into hospital on Christmas Day. She's not in pain, but her legs don't seem to do what she wants them to.

Mum isn't very tall – just 160 centimetres – and weighs 43 kilos. She has blue eyes, thick brown hair and never gets cross. She was 19 when she had me.

Dad goes over to the mainland every day to see her. When he comes back he doesn't say much, but his right leg shakes more than normal when we have supper. I can feel the floor shaking.

When Mum comes home a week later, she has got crutches. She is 28 years old and something isn't quite right, but they don't know what.

EVERY MORNING I GO over the hill to school; it takes me two minutes. I have a blue backpack with a piece of fruit in it. I walk backwards waving to Mum until I can't see her any longer in the kitchen window.

The schoolhouse is old and run-down, the floor slopes and my pencil rolls away if I drop it. My teacher Ingrid Bjerger has got red lipstick that often leaves smears on her teeth. She smokes, but she always smells nice.

'Markus, run three times around the school and I'll time you,' she says.

That is one of her ways of calming me down. My legs are always itching and I find it difficult to sit still. At breaktime we play football and I tease the older boys just so that I can feel the excitement of being chased.

Öckerö, the island where Mum's family has lived for generations, lies in the archipelago between Vinga and Marstrand north of Gothenburg. It is one of two communities in Sweden not connected to the mainland. The island isn't big; there are cars, but you can get everywhere just walking or cycling. To the west lies the open sea with a horizon that never ends. To the east is Gothenburg, and the lights from the city light up the sky when it's dark.

Öckerö has still got some places that are uninhabited, but not many. The houses stand close together. Ours is big; Dad built it on Grandma and Grandad's land where the cows used to graze long ago. The only thing that separates the two plots is a steel fence, painted black, which Grandad has concreted into the bedrock. Me and my siblings used to clamber on it and hang upside down.

Our house is built of brown bricks with a rough surface, and the roof is covered in dark concrete tiles smeared in birdshit. The seagulls love to sit there screeching. Almost every day I climb up a drainpipe, pull myself up across the gutter and sit down on the roof to keep watch. I stay there until Mum shouts for me to come down.

The others and I have our own bedrooms on the top floor. In the basement we have a big open fireplace. Two brothers from the neighbouring island of Fotö built it and also the foundation of the house. Dad says that he came back from a building site one day after work to see what was happening, and one of the brothers was just doing the fireplace and Dad thought it looked all crooked. He wondered if it was really meant to look like that.

'It's good enough for townspeople,' he was told.

I AM 10 and have entered my first race: the Ö-circuit (island-circuit), 10 kilometres of asphalt. I jog the 500 metres across the hill to the covered ice rink where the race will start. My uncle and my cousin, who's two years older than me, are also lined up at the start.

I'm wearing plimsolls, a pair of pink shorts and a T-shirt. Mum, Dad and my siblings have come to watch. Mum wonders whether it's a good idea – isn't it a bit too much for a 10-year-old?

We're off. My cousin and I stick together, and we soon leave my uncle behind.

Kilometre after kilometre passes, and everything seems fine. We run through the streets of Öckerö, side by side, my cousin and I. Neither of us wants to slow down. I guess he doesn't want to be beaten by his younger cousin and I just want to keep up.

I just run, I don't think, I just take one step at a time. I've never run this far before.

The finishing line is getting close. We put on a spurt and my legs hurt. It feels as if they aren't quite part of me.

My cousin and I are separated by one second at the end – my time is 44 minutes 4 seconds, and my cousin's 44 minutes 3 seconds.

I sit down in the shade along the wall of the ice rink. My legs are twitching as if they are separate from me. The nerves seem to have a life of their own and I can't do anything about it.

I am getting a nosebleed. I can feel the salt from the sweat on my forehead making my skin feel stiff and there's a taste of iron as the blood runs down my throat.

What a feeling!

SUNDAY MORNING IN CHURCH. The time moves slowly. Grandma and Grandad are sitting a few pews behind us. Mum is at home on the sofa. I hear Grandad's voice when we sing. He loves the old hymns.

I find them quite difficult. They go so high and I don't dare even try to hit those high notes. I don't like to hear my own voice. I don't know if I'm singing off-key. It's better to keep quiet.

During the sermon my legs start twitching, the same feeling I get sitting at my desk at school. What am I doing here?

The preacher uses words I don't understand. He talks about the end of the world, saying that God will come and separate the just from the unjust, that children will turn against their parents and that the world will perish in flames.

MUM IS LYING UNDER her blanket and she's crying. Grandma is with her. I hear them through the wall.

Mum refuses to come out. She has read the big green medical book and says that she now knows what's wrong, why she has problems with her balance and why her body doesn't do what she wants it to.

'I have MS. I have all the symptoms. I have had inflammation of my optic nerve, my legs are numb and I've suffered from loss of feeling in my arms since I was a little girl. I have a body that just doesn't respond and I've got problems with my balance.'

When Dad comes home from work, he gets angry. He takes the big, fat book and hides it.

He doesn't want Mum to read any more, we don't know if it really is MS. The doctors haven't made any proper diagnosis.

There's no point in jumping to any conclusions.

WHEN I START middle school, I have to move to Ankaret, a yellow wooden building down by the port. It takes five minutes to cycle there and five to run.

It is next to the high school and we share a dining room with the older pupils. I tease them too. I can't help myself. I love being pursued by the high-school boys, to feel that they are getting closer and will beat me up if they catch me. It is serious. The rush I feel when I just about manage to escape makes it possible for me to keep still until the next breaktime.

My new teacher is called Ingrid. She has grey hair and usually wears a cardigan. I write in such tiny letters that she has to read my words with a magnifying glass. My stories are always about blood and death.

IN 1988 I AM TWELVE and I run my second race. This time the sports club has changed the circuit to include both Öckerö and the neighbouring island, Hälsö.

I have played more ice hockey, run more and played more football, so I am stronger than last time. I've got proper sports shoes and I've borrowed my dad's running shorts, a pair of smart, synthetic shorts in the colours of the national team. Neither my uncle nor my cousin are taking part, so I can run my own race.

I start out fast; my body responds and I keep up the speed. I run without a watch. I'm just following my body's signals. It hurts, but it works.

I like the pounding feeling in my chest and my breathing is deep. As long as it is, I will not get that numb feeling. I have learned that in the last couple of years, to stay on the right side of the boundary. I finish in just over 38 minutes and am really pleased.

ONE SUNDAY I MISS the revival meeting. And that isn't good. I can feel it inside me. Everyone I know was there, but I was playing ice hockey.

Egon Sandström was the preacher that day. My mates learned to speak in tongues and I missed it. The members of the congregation fell to the ground through the power of the Holy Spirit.

Our pastor isn't amused: 'Markus, you must choose. Which path do you want, the narrow one or the wide one? The one that leads to heaven, or the one that leads to hell? You have to decide.'

ONE SUMMER'S EVENING I GO with Grandad to catch mackerel. Grandad was 17 the first time he sailed for seven days through heavy fog to Iceland to fish, and he has been a fisherman ever since. He's short and sturdy and his hair is as white as sugar. He is agile despite his weight and has big feet – Grandma says this is so that he can stand firm on deck when the waves are high.

Grandad is good to have around when something needs demolishing, says Dad. For more delicate carpentry, he's not that good. Everything has to happen fast, and if a wooden stud is a bit too long he doesn't saw it off, he takes the sledgehammer and gives it a good bashing.

He can easily cut down a newly planted shrub, explaining that he thought it was a weed. Then Grandma chases him round the garden with a stick.

He looks at everything the way he looks at a new catch of fish that needs sorting. It has to be done quickly, some is discarded and chucked back, and everything will be fine as long as you make a proper effort. Grandad is solid. Screaming grandchildren or boys with legs that need to run are no problem for him.

When my cousins and I climb up some tall tree and a worried adult thinks that we are going to fall down and break our legs, Grandad says: 'It's no big deal.'

We leave port around eight in the evening. The sun is up and the air is mild. Grandad's brother is also there. The brothers are complete opposites. Grandad's eyes are blue, his brother's are brown. Grandad thinks that everything will be fine, while his brother is more careful and has a tin for every sort of screw.

When they were young and owned Öckerö's first iron-hulled boat, Grandad was the skipper and his brother looked after the engine. It was probably a good division of labour: a fearless skipper and a meticulous mechanic.

We pass Hälsö and reach the open sea. The cabin stinks of diesel and engine oil, and I begin to feel queasy from the smells and the movement of the sea. Grandad laughs when I vomit for the first time.

'It will pass,' he says.

The heaving sensation in my gut briefly disappears but soon returns. There are many hours to go before we get back home. First we have to get to the place where we set the nets, and then we have to go very slowly southwards for hour after hour until it's time to pull the nets back in.

Why do I never learn? Why do I go with them when I am always so seasick?

After I've been sick for the tenth time, I lie down in the hold on a damp mattress. There I stay in a state of restless sleep, until Grandad shouts that it's time to pull up the nets, time to go up on deck and help out.

Now it is dark, the lamps on the deck are lit. We pull up length after length, pull out the fish and put them on a layer of ice. After an hour's work it's all done and we turn homewards.

The pier moves under my feet when I jump onto it, everything is spinning. Grandad and I cycle home just as dawn is breaking, he to his house, and I to mine.

WE NOW KNOW EXACTLY what is wrong. Mum has had her diagnosis: multiple sclerosis.

This illness of the nervous system means that the signals from the brain to the muscles don't work the way they're meant to. That means that the muscles are getting weaker, which in turn means that any physical movement becomes harder. MS tends to relapse: the body gets worse at certain times and improves a little in between.

But it doesn't have to be so serious, say the doctors. You can get different types of MS. Some are more aggressive while others are gentler. Time will show which sort Mum has got.

In the evenings, when she goes upstairs to say evening prayers with my siblings and me, Dad or one of us has to help her. Most often it's me.

In the evenings Dad is usually down in the basement doing his accounts. He works selling office equipment, copiers and typewriters. The company is called Torgeby's Office Supplies and is based in the old town in Gothenburg, next door to SKF, the ballbearing company.

Dad is good at selling; he's honest and straight and people like that. Dad took over from his father when he died of bowel cancer. I was four when he died and barely remember him.

My sisters are like two sides of the same coin. Elin is dark with green eyes. She is very lively in the evening and almost dead in the morning. She looks like Dad. Ida is tired in the evening and very lively in the morning, and she's the only one in the family who's blonde. Dad calls her Skorpan.

Every evening Mum shouts for help at the bottom of the stairs and then we pray: 'God who holds the children dear, look after me, your little one . . .'

Mum can no longer go out when it's windy, as she might be blown over. She can't work any more and has been given sick leave from her job as a medical secretary at Lillhagens hospital in Gothenburg. She can no longer make her hands write.

16

Instead she lies on the sofa crying.

Grandma spends time with her every day. I hear them from a distance. Mum is worried about what will happen.

'Who will take care of the children when I no longer can?'

Grandad takes in the paper every morning. I hear him humming as he walks through the garage. He doesn't say a lot, he just watches in silence.

Mum is 30 years old and her body is starting to run down.

I find it really difficult that Mum cries so much, but I don't know what to do. I just feel frustrated.

She is starting to use a wheelchair.

I HAVE FINISHED MIDDLE SCHOOL and have moved on to the final two years at a new school called Bratteberg. It feels dry and barren; hard concrete corridors with numbered lockers along the walls. I can't cope with sitting inside, I want to get out. I don't do any homework, I'm unmotivated and my head feels heavy.

My legs are itching so hard that I can't sit still on a chair.

PE is the only subject that works for me. Maybe I'm just a bit stupid?

When I come home from school, Mum is resting on the sofa and her eyes are red from crying. One of the carers has been there and cleaned and there are meatballs on the stove. They are small and round, not the way Mum used to make them. They taste different.

I just blurt out: 'Why don't you stop crying? I don't want to hear your whingeing any more.'

I go down to ICA, the supermarket where I work as an errand boy every other week. I look after the dairy section and get 30 kronor [$3.50] an hour. Sometimes when I'm hungry I happen to break a yoghurt carton, which I immediately gulp down there and then in the cool storage area.

AT THE END OF THE YEAR I am picked to take part in the national school athletics championships. I am going to run the 3000 metres at the Stockholm stadium.

I get up early to take the ferry and then the bus to Heden to catch the coach to Stockholm. The only one I know on the journey is Per-Fredrik, a mate from neighbouring island Hönö.

He is Sweden's best pole-vaulter. We know each other from the ice hockey team. I go skating or hockey training 20 hours a week. That's what I do when I'm not at school or working at ICA.

This is my first time in Stockholm and I am stressed out because I can't see any further than the next house. No horizon. Everything is so close to me and moves so fast.

This is the first time that I am going to run on a track. I jog two laps to warm up; the tarmac feels hard and soft at the same time – I have never felt anything like it. I am used to hard rocks and asphalt.

I've borrowed Dad's running shoes, a pair of heavy Nikes with cushioned heels. I am wearing white football shorts and a vest he had when he ran the Gothenburg circuit.

The other runners have race vests and shorts in matching colours, and proper running shoes with spikes. This is the first time I've seen spikes. The shoes look thin and light.

From the start the boys in spikes run a bit cagily; they glance at each other. I don't get what they are up to. If you are in a race, surely it is good to run as fast as you can. The few times I have been in a race, I have always started out as fast as I could.

I'm in the lead and stay there for a couple of laps with my heavy running shoes and football shorts. My self-confidence grows. The people are shouting, it feels as if everyone is looking at me. I hear my name through the loudspeakers: 'Markus Torgeby from Öckerö is in the lead!'

The others are behind me. I feel great and I push on as hard as I can. When there are two laps remaining, the more experienced runners get going. I have to let them pass me at once and they fly by on fresh legs. Metre after metre. I make the maximum possible effort, but it's no use; the distance between me and the others just grows and grows.

I am among the last to cross the line in 9 minutes 50 seconds, 150 metres behind the winner.

My disappointment at not having measured up takes over my whole body. I feel that everyone in the stadium is staring at me.

THE FATHER OF ONE OF my mates in the ice hockey team keeps telling me that I should concentrate on running. He thinks that I should start training seriously with a club in town.

'Markus, running comes easily to you,' he says. 'In training runs you easily outrun the others. And it's obvious you like it. You're more of a lone wolf and I think that running is your thing.'

The summer after leaving school, I meet a really good runner from another neighbouring island, Björkö, who is a couple of years older than me. We decide to meet at the Slottsskogsvallen sports centre the following day.

I cycle to the ferry, catch the 24 bus to the central station and then the tram to Slottsskogen. An hour and 40 minutes later, I'm there.

We meet outside the entrance to the athletics block. Alongside two other runners we warm up by running the four-kilometre circuit around Slottsskogen. I've never run here before and it's good to run among trees. It smells different. On Öckerö there are hardly any trees.

We're going to run intervals around Azaleadalen, a large field in Slottsskogen: eight runs of 820 metres, with 90 seconds between each lap.

This is my first time interval running and I don't know what to expect, only that I must run as fast as I can. We're off, the other boys are pressing hard. My legs are sore and the grass saps my strength.

At the end of the first lap, I'm 20 metres behind. I'm tired, but it feels OK. We carry on, interval after interval. I'm 20 metres behind every time, but no more than that. I get more and more tired, but only up to a certain point. After the training I feel happy.

We do a warm-down jog and carry on to the athletics block to shower and change. The runner from Björkö tells me that he doesn't have a trainer and that he doesn't know how long he's going to carry on running.

'I train with my mates because it's a laugh, but I think you should start working with a trainer.'

He nods towards a man in the corner: 'Do you see the chap with the short dark hair? He's a running coach for Örgryte. I don't like him, he's too harsh and shouts too much, but he may suit you.' [Örgryte is a well-known sports club.]

I'm introduced to the trainer, and we decide that I'll come back at 4.30 p.m. the next day to do my first session with the group.

WHEN I ARRIVE THE NEXT DAY, the famous high-jumper Patrik Sjöberg is standing outside smoking, leaning casually against a little sports car. Inside, in the athletics block I go past the high-jump mats where scrawny fellows are listening to a trainer speaking in a strange Swedish accent, and past the throwing circle where muscular guys and girls are doing their stretching exercises. Everyone is focused on what they are doing.

The coach and the other runners are waiting at the bend where they always meet up before training. I'm introduced: a thin, blonde girl is younger than me, while the others are boys a year or so older than me.

I feel a bit stupid, everyone is looking at me.

'We are going to do interval training in the Änggårdsbergen,' says the coach. Twelve times 400 metres on a hilly circuit, with 60 seconds of rest between each one.

We warm up by running to the start. We do some stretching and a few sprints before it's time to start.

'Three, two, one, go!' shouts the coach, and everyone sets off at a terrific pace.

I'm keeping up really well and the more intervals we run, the better it feels. I realise that this might be my strong point, not speed but stamina.

When we're done we run back to the athletics building, and round off with some strengthening exercises. Before I go off to get changed, the coach says, 'Markus, it's the 800 metres regional championships in two weeks. I think you should enter. You can borrow my running spikes. See you tomorrow.'

THE COMPETITION IS at Slottsskogsvallen. Gunder Hägg set his world records here in the 1940s, in hard-fought battles against Örgryte's Arne Andersson. Thousands were there cheering them on. At the regional championships 50 years later, the gravel has been replaced by red Tartan track, and the stands are empty.

I put on my coach's running spikes. It's an extraordinary sensation to have them on my feet. I can hardly feel them. It's like running barefoot.

The organiser blows his whistle signalling the start, and I am in lane five. In the lane to the left is Edin Alivodic, the Swedish junior champion in the 1500 metres steeplechase. He is the favourite.

I've no idea how it will work out. I only know that 800 metres is a short distance and it will be fast right from the start.

We're off and I am right on Edin's shoulder. We're going fast. After 400 metres I'm tired, but I still have some energy left. I'm really close to Edin. I refuse to ease off.

Two hundred metres to go and I am still there, while the others are starting to fall away. With 100 metres to go, Edin changes gear, but I'm sticking with him like a leech.

At the finish I am two metres behind.

After the race, I walk about coughing: my throat and lungs aren't used to such fast and intensive breathing. The coach is super-happy. Me too – my first 800-metre race and I manage to stick with it all the way! Soon it will be my back that the others will be looking at.

I have butterflies in my stomach. This is what I will do in life. It's so simple.

A MONTH LATER I am sitting on the coach from Gothenburg to Falun to run in my first national championship. The whole coach is packed with young people from different Gothenburg clubs. We are all between 16 and 18 years old. Almost all the faces are new to me.

The pole-vaulters' poles are lying down the central aisle and I am told not to step on them. All the pole-vaulters themselves are sitting together in their own part of the coach playing cards. The sprinters and jumpers are sitting together, and the throwers are sitting on their own.

It's easy to see who does which event: the tall, lanky high jumpers with their hair slicked back; big, spotty throwers with headphones. The pole-vaulters are the liveliest, they never stop talking.

I'm going to run the 3000 metres for boys aged 16. It's a tough group with a lot of good runners who have been in training for years. I don't know if I'm ready, but the coach thinks that I should go, even if he stays home himself.

We are travelling the day before the race and check into a cheap hotel. In the evening I go out and have some Chinese food with the pole-vaulters and their coach. They talk about different poles, and at what height they will enter the competition. Myself, I haven't got a clue about anything – everything is new to me.

On the day of the competition I wake up with the butterflies in my stomach again. I feel seriously charged up and ready to go.

The start is getting closer. I warm up and do some quick sprints. I am wearing my coach's spikes. There are a lot of people in the stands and around the track.

As I stand on the starting line I feel like I am in the right place. I am going to give everything. If anyone is going to run faster than I will, they are going to have to run seriously fast.

We're off and the pace is quick, but after a lap or so it calms down a bit and I decide to run up and take the lead. I run as hard as can. With two laps to go some of them fall behind, but the best are sticking with the pace. The bell rings for the last lap, and we are getting closer to the final spurt. I have nothing left to give and finish fourth, three seconds behind the winner.

I am deeply disappointed, but I still feel that this is my thing. To stand on the starting line with Sweden's best runners next to me and with the attitude that I will be hard to beat. That is a fantastic feeling.

MY COACH DRINKS a lot of coffee. Always the same brand, Löfbergs Lila, out of a thermos in a white plastic mug. He works nights and he often looks really tired.

He is really clear and straight and precise in what he says: what speed I should run the intervals, how long the breaks should be. I like being instructed. I don't need to think, just do what the coach says.

I want to be in a physical world. Everything simple and concrete.

Mum's tears don't exist. Everything is about running.

Life has clarity.

MY SECOND NATIONAL championship: 1500 metres for boys aged 18.

The contest is indoors in the athletics arena on tracks where I train every day. It is February and cold outside. I have eight months of serious training in my body now. I've got more muscles and I'm tougher.

Mum and Dad have come to watch, Mum in her wheelchair, her head falling forward, and Dad at her side, supporting her.

Before I start to warm up for the final, my coach sits down next to me. He tries to pep me up, saying: 'Markus, today there is just one lad who can win this, and that's you. Nobody else.'

That cheers me up. But it also makes me nervous. My arms feel heavier and the bubbles are growing in my chest. How can he possibly know that I am the only one who can win?

The place is packed out. The air feels heavy and full of anxiety. I find it hard to sit still.

All the competitors are looking to gee themselves up in their various ways, some chatting nervously, others lying down in a corner listening to music through their headphones. I walk out into the trees in Slottsskogen, where I warm up on my own in a place that is colder and quieter. A few minutes before the start I jog back and quickly change into my spikes.

I am on the starting line. This is when it counts.

The starting pistol rings out and we are off. We are going to run seven-and-a-half-laps of a 200-metre track. Everything seems to be working well, my body responds and I feel strong.

With one lap remaining I take over the lead and I give it my all. When there are 50 metres left I am still in the lead, everything will be fine, I'm about to win. Shit, this is big stuff!

I am first over the line and raise my arms. I have won my first Swedish championships.

Then I hear the bell signalling that I have one more lap to go.

I start to run again, but my legs are heavy and full of lactic acid. At last the legs start moving and I stagger over the line in eighth place.

What happened? How could I miss a whole lap? It's not as if I was so tired that my brain was disconnected from my body.

I go up to Mum and Dad.

'Things don't always work out,' says Dad. 'There will be other races.'

I meet up with my coach in the stands. He doesn't say a word.

Afterwards, Mum, Dad and I go to the car. Dad lifts Mum into the front seat and helps her with the seat belt.

We go to the Sjuans street café on Vasagatan for a milkshake. 'The best in town,' says Dad. I have a chocolate shake and don't feel too good afterwards.

When we get home I have to go out for a run.

I AM SUCKED INTO TRAINING. It's like some dormant need that has finally found release.

I put all my restlessness and anxiety into my running and I run until my legs scream and my lungs hurt. In my running there are no thoughts, only deep breaths and my legs and a rhythm that calms me down.

I do what my coach says, and a bit more. More is better.

Early in the mornings, I take the ferry and bus into town to train before I go to the athletic college in Frölunda. I spend the whole day at school, and then train some more. I take the bus to the ferry and walk the last four kilometres back home.

Sometimes I borrow Grandad's bike without asking and leave it down by the ferry. Quite often I forget the lock and so I have to hide it in some shrubs a few hundred metres away. Sometimes it's gone when I get back.

Grandma is always furious: 'Markus, now you better find Grandad's bike!'

Grandma is not at all pretty when she's cross. Why don't I learn to lock up the bike? I know what happens when it's gone.

I have to run round the island to track it down.

When I come home at night, my legs are heavy and there's a hollow feeling in my stomach. I haven't eaten since lunch. My brain feels slower and I need something sweet.

Mum is already in bed. She is tired and resting on her front. I lie down next to her for a short while, something that I do every evening. This is our time.

We chat about the day, what has happened and what we are longing for. Mum is longing to be well. Longing for God to make her legs strong again.

'I don't want to lie here anymore. It's boring. I want to get out.'

I eat muesli and drink some pop. My body feels sluggish after a long day.

I am already looking forward to the next training session.

I DO A CROSS-COUNTRY race in Eksjö – four kilometres on the same excellent grass course that the Swedish cross-country championship will be run on a few weeks later. I push myself hard from the very first step. My coach is screaming at the top of his voice right by the side of the track. Everything seems to flow and I win easily.

When I get to the finish line, my coach is pleased: 'Markus, this is really promising for the national cross-country race. We're aiming for the podium.'

I feel a knot in my stomach.

Then there's really tough interval training on grass in Azaleadalen followed by long intervals in the Änggårdsbergen. All this to keep improving my form. Day after day.

Four weeks later, we're back in Eksjö. I begin my warm-up.

'This is it, Markus,' says my coach.

I'm nervous. I feel heavy.

I change into my racing shoes, a pair of light Reeboks with 15mm spikes, and put on my racing top in the blue and red of Örgryte.

We are spread out on a long line, the other runners and I. The starting pistol is fired and it's full steam ahead at once. But my legs feel dead, they just don't work. I try as hard as I can, but they simply don't work.

My coach is screaming: 'Come on now, Markus!'

Nothing helps. It's as if my legs were filled with cement. I come in way behind the winner, and feel embarrassed. What am I doing? What sort of a weak person am I who can't run fast when it matters?

I just want to go back home, get out there and punish myself with a really hard session of interval running.

Just to forget everything.

MUM SITS SLUMPED in her wheelchair, talking on the telephone. She needs both hands to hold the receiver. Her arms are trembling.

It's probably Per-Olof. He's got a drinking problem and often calls Mum when things are going badly.

Mum mainly listens. She's too tired to talk much. Instead she has to speak in a special way, to say a lot with only a few words.

It's not always easy to understand her.

Spring has come and I'm restless. I want to go out into the sun, up into the hills and find a sheltered rock out of the wind. I want to be alone.

Mum asks if I can draw the curtain. She always wants it to be just so. Nothing annoys me more than to have to open or close the curtains in this particular way. Every day the same problem with the curtains.

I know that she asks me because she can't do it herself, but I still get angry: 'Mum, I don't give a shit about your curtains! I can't be bothered.'

Mum starts crying. I go out.

I AM GOING TO RUN 1500 metres in Mölndal. I don't feel like it. As soon as I push myself, my legs seem to seize up.

We are starting to train more on the track instead, and I run intervals every day apart from Sundays.

The coach is on my case: 'Markus, it's good for you to compete. Why are you training if you don't want to compete? That's what it's all about, isn't it? You run fast in training and then it's time to show that when you race.'

When he says that, I can feel black butterflies fluttering in my chest.

My legs get heavier the closer we get to the race. I go to the toilet several times a day. I can't keep the food down. Everything comes out unprocessed.

I find it difficult to breathe. Every breath feels really shallow. I want to train harder, but I have completely lost the desire to push myself.

I have nosebleeds every day. I'm sure I've got leukaemia.

On the starting line I know it's all going to go to pot. My whole body is full of lactic acid even before I set off.

I don't want to be here. I want to run on my own out in the hills.

'Come on, Markus, this is it!' shouts my coach.

After the first lap I am one second behind the leader, and my anxiety makes my legs feel heavy. My coach shouts: 'Keep in touch! Don't fall back! Push harder!'

After two laps I'm three seconds behind. No energy. My body's all stiff.

I stagger over the finishing line.

'What's going on, Markus?' asks my coach. 'You actually run faster in training.'

'I don't know what it is,' I say, 'I'm just tired.'

'Markus, I know that you can run faster than you did today. If you are going to take part in the nationals, it would be a good idea to start performing in the actual races now. We're doing intervals again tomorrow. See you then.'

THE FOOTBALL WORLD CUP is starting in the US, and the heat of the Swedish summer is breaking records. The family is going on a two-week boating holiday and I am going with them. 'There's no alternative,' says Dad. 'We don't know how long Mum will be able to go on a boat, so we have to take the chance while we can.'

I would rather stay at home. Two weeks without any proper training is no good. My coach isn't pleased that I'm going away for two weeks in the middle of the season.

I'm stuck in the middle between two strong-willed people. But for Dad there's no room for discussion.

We sail north along the west coast, up past Lysekil towards the Koster islands. The boat is 32 feet long, so there is plenty of room for a family with four children.

The wheelchair is folded up in the stern. Dad is at the helm with Mum sitting next to him.

All is nice and calm. We go ashore wherever we want. We swim and I do 70 metres underwater and jump in from high rocks. Dad goes waterskiing, falls backwards with his legs wide apart. Mum laughs so hard she cries.

Back home I feel completely rested. On the Monday I'm back in training. 'On Thursday you're going to run a trial for the 2000 metre steeplechase,' says my coach afterwards.

I do stretches before heading home. I've done some steeplechase training earlier on, but I've never done a race with the water and everything. I still think it might be fun. I don't remember when I last felt like this.

On the Thursday I warm up and do my sprints. My whole body responds. Everything seems easy.

I am ready when my coach says it's time to go.

Alone against the clock and I know it will all work out.

I'm off; the laps go by and there's no fatigue at all. I have never experienced anything like this.

After five laps I finish with a time of 5 minutes 50 seconds.

The time is taken manually and it's only a test run, so it will never be recognised. But I know that no other Swedish runner in my age group has run the race any faster this year.

THE TRAINER IS ECSTATIC. Finally we have got it right. Steeplechase is my thing.

I am put in for my first steeplechase event – the 3000-metre district championship back in Gothenburg.

On the day of the race I warm up by running the long lap in Slottsskogen, past Azaleadalen, towards the natural history museum, four kilometres of easy jogging and some sprints. Then I put on my spikes and it's time to go.

Ahmed Mohamed is also on the starting line. He's one of the best junior steeplechasers in Sweden.

We're off. This is where I want to be. Excited but relaxed.

We run lap after lap together, side by side. We're both fast and cross the finishing line together.

My coach comes straight up to me and tells me that I have the chance to qualify for the junior European championships the next summer. His eyes are shining: 'You only need to knock off a few seconds and that won't be a problem. You've got a whole year, and this was the first time you've run a 3000-metre steeplechase. Just remember that, Markus. There are plenty of details that you can improve on.'

I SECURE MUM in her wheelchair with a strap, and put on my rollerblades. I lean the wheelchair backwards so that the front wheels don't touch the ground. The resistance becomes less then and the chair doesn't vibrate so much at speed. Then we're off.

We do one lap around Öckerö, first to the Hönöbron, then up over the steep Kandalsliabacken and from there straight to Hälsöbron. Downhill our speed reaches 40km/h. The strap across Mum's stomach stops her from falling out when I have to brake.

At top speed her hair is blown back by the wind and I can feel its thick strands tickling my nose. Mum is not afraid. She loves the speed.

I BRUSH MUM'S TEETH. She can no longer hold the toothbrush, her hands shake too much. Dad has bought an electric toothbrush that we use.

I am tired and I get a nosebleed.

I've got a maths test and I don't understand how the numbers hang together. They are like a kind of fog. I think I am probably a bit stupid.

In my room I do 200 press-ups and 200 sit-ups instead. That takes five minutes, and I do it every evening before going to sleep.

Then I open the window and turn off the radiator. My body is warm at night.

I lie down in bed with my head against the headboard. I want to feel pressure at the top of my head. I fall asleep more quickly that way.

I AM SITTING ON the morning bus on the way to town and I hate feeling hemmed in. School doesn't work for me. My brain feels like molasses.

But first I need to go to Slottsskogen for my training. I change in the athletics building, and do some distance running on my own in the Änggårdsbergen. First through the Botanic Gardens, then upwards.

From up there you get a good view of Gothenburg: the Älvsborgsbron to the west, and on the other side of the river you can see the crane at Eriksberg [the legacy of its former shipyards], and beyond that the archipelago and the sea. I can see the cars on the Särö road and hear the squeaking of the trams. This is where I want to be. This has eased the pressure in my brain. I don't give a shit about being an hour late for school. I just don't care, it's not important.

As soon as I get off the train at Frölunda market and start walking towards school, my legs feel like they are filled with rocks. They get heavier and heavier the closer I get to school.

I don't understand why I should be stuck inside doing something I don't want to do. I don't bother with any homework and always have the lowest marks in the class in every test.

I just want to run.

THE FATHER OF AN OLD GIRLFRIEND of mine gives me a copy of *Walden*.

'Here you are,' he says. 'I think this is for you.'

The book reaches straight into my heart. The author writes of all the things that I've been thinking about: the simple and concrete things, the stuff that you feel in your body. All that I experience and wonder about when I am running. Things that I have never spoken about to anyone else.

He writes about the year when he lived in a cottage by a lake. About nature. The forest, the lakes, the grass and the seasons. How the crops grow, and what he wears.

I am considering doing something like that. Moving away somewhere and seeing how that affects me.

ONE DAY AFTER the afternoon training session, I am standing on my own waiting for the tram for Marklandsgatan. I am in my own bubble, thinking about the sea and how it rolls along in the wind. I've got Mazzy Star playing in my headphones.

A group of boys comes towards me. They surround me.

'You get that you're dumb, don't you?' says a short kid with greasy black hair.

'What do you mean?' I say.

'Don't fuck around, you bastard. You are dumb. Say it!'

'You want me to say I'm dumb?'

'Exactly. Just say it. Otherwise we'll kick the shit out of you.'

I want to smack that little prick in the mouth, but there are too many of them.

'OK, I'm dumb.'

They are laughing at me.

'What have you got?' says the greasy kid.

'Just a bus pass.'

'No money?'

'Nah.'

The tram they want arrives.

'You're in luck, you bastard. Next time we'll get you.'

When they've got into the tram and the doors have closed, I give them the finger through the window.

WINTER TRAINING, thousand-metre slopes in the Änggårds- bergen, something I do once a week. I like tackling the hills; there's no rest when you run uphill, the effort is constant.

Last week's average was 3 minutes 8 seconds per kilometre. Then I felt completely wiped out.

I don't want to do worse now, but I don't think I can manage a faster time.

The air is damp. I run in a vest and long tights, bareheaded, and only thin gloves. I'm going to go for eight uphill runs, and the rest periods are the kilometre-long jogs back down to the start.

My coach stands at the bottom of the hill. He wants to know the time for each interval.

I run off and my body doesn't respond. My breathing is forced. Hard and deep breaths, which I feel in my breastbone. I try to keep my shoulders down. My body is dead. I get a time of 3 minutes 10 seconds for the first interval.

I'm sliding backwards, I'm worse than last week. I'm a loser.

I try to run faster, but I can't push myself. I've ground to a halt.

I don't want to report the time to my coach, but I do it anyway. I'm not measuring up. I want to give it all up.

It feels heavier and heavier, and the average for the eight hills is 3 minutes 14 seconds.

I'VE GOT THIS HEAVINESS in my body that just won't ease up. An anxiety that is lodged there, which I can't really reach.

I'm tired, but even so I do a double session every day. I'm always hungry, but I don't eat.

I am beginning to get the same symptoms as Mum before she got really ill: heavy legs and a feeling that my body doesn't respond. My legs are numb and I've got pins and needles in my feet. It's hard to go upstairs, I get breathless.

I can't fight the dark thoughts when they come: I am about to get sick like Mum.

The ghosts in my head pop up when I least expect them: on the bus, when I'm in bed and want to go to sleep, at school. When they arrive, my breathing gets shallow, I don't get enough oxygen, my arms stiffen up, I'm afraid.

My head feels like a tumble dryer.

Dad and I fight. We clash every evening when I get back from training. I'm careless, leave my clothes all over the place, don't hang up my wet towels. They go mouldy and smell bad.

Dad is raging, he has better things to do than clear up after me.

I understand him, but I can't change. I haven't got enough energy to sort myself out.

I just can't.

I want to ease all that pressure, but I don't know how. Up there in my head there's this constant grinding.

The only time it's quiet is when I do the intense interval training or run alone on the rocks of Öckerö.

SPRING TURNS INTO SUMMER, school finishes and I start a summer job with the council. My task is to keep the beaches clear of seaweed. From seven in the morning until two in the afternoon I drive around the islands, working away with a pitchfork. It's heavy going, but I can be outside all the time in the sun and the wind. I can look at the sea every day, listen to the way it sounds depending on where the wind is coming from.

I can be fully inside my body and work until I'm dripping with sweat.

I eat breakfast outside, sitting on the rocks. I see the way the sun makes the sea change colour. I do some distance running before I get back to work.

I run along the cliff on the west side of Öckerö, across heather and rocks, jumping over crevices in long strides. All on my own, no one around. There's thunder in the air, the heat is oppressive. There are dark blue rain clouds over the city.

I run out to Rävholmen, passing the sandy beach where I used to swim as a child, when Mum could still walk. I run across the hills to Jakobsspratt, a rocky outcrop. I look over the edge and can't see anything below. I step back, take a run-up and then jump.

I fly through the air. My stomach tightens.

I land in the water 13 metres below.

I swim in my running clothes, shoes and all, over the strait to Hönö, 400 metres' gentle breaststroke. I carry on running on the other side, along the little coves all the way to the other side of the island. I'm not tired. Vinga lighthouse is a couple of kilometres away. The boats are coming in with the night's catch.

I carry on towards Fotö, running across the bridge. Great views in all directions. I see the cranes in Gothenburg. The morning sun. The horizon.

I run past the old port and the ice-cream stand. My legs are getting a bit numb from the hard road surface and I turn back homewards. I get back with a slight salty, chafing feeling between my legs.

My head feels light, my body clean and pure.

In the evenings after work I take the bus into town to train. The bus is warm and clammy, full of people who are going to Gothenburg to just hang out.

When I come back after training I take late-evening swims. I jump from the rocks that are still warm from the sun. I swim underwater, deep down in the darkness, counting the strokes to see how far I am going. The deeper I go, the stronger the pressure I feel across my chest. When it gets too much, I turn back up to the surface. The pressure eases with every stroke. I take a deep breath at the surface. The sense of calm returns.

Born again. I don't want to be anywhere but here. By the sea, on the warm granite.

I don't shower, swimming is enough. My hair is stiff with salt.

WHEN THE HEAT OF SUMMER reaches its peak, life is hard for Mum. The illness has made her sensitive to heat; her body's thermostat doesn't work. She has to use a cooling vest to bring down her body temperature.

Mum lies in the shade, longing to get out; I can see it. She wants to swim, to cool down. To feel the salt on her face.

I ask her if she wants to come along for a swim.

'Absolutely,' she replies.

She hasn't been swimming for many years, but what does that matter? I help her put on her swimsuit and we take the wheelchair down to the beach by Bagglebo. Mum is still really light, in spite of sitting in the wheelchair for all these years. It's no effort to carry her down the steps to the water.

It is shallow, so I can walk out. I cradle her head so that she can float on her back.

Her whole body twitches when the nerves come into contact with the cold water. Her body seems to have a life of its own. After a couple of minutes her body temperature has gone down by a few degrees. Everything becomes easier for her, to talk, to move.

Afterwards I carry her up to the beach. She's stiff as a board and very happy.

I'm happy too. I'm good at this, swimming with Mum who doesn't go swimming so often, and whose legs twitch and behave as they please.

DURING THE WORLD ATHLETICS CHAMPIONSHIPS in Gothenburg, Jonathan Edwards breaks the triple jump world record. My mate Johan and I take the evening bus into Gothenburg. The whole city is crammed with people; every pavement café is packed out and you can hardly make your way along the Avenue.

We go up to the Götaplatsen, the famous city square, and sneak in between the houses. We get undressed and hide our clothes under some shrubs. The only thing I'm wearing is my shoes, a pair of blue Pumas. There we stand, naked behind the houses, plucking up the courage. Johan is slightly pissed.

Then we jog out onto the Götaplatsen, and when we get up to the statue of Poseidon we pick up speed. We run along the tram tracks to Brunnsparken. Our willies slap against our legs. Johan is running a few steps behind me.

The people on the Avenue scream and point. We run between a pair of patrolling police officers. They haven't time to react before they see our pale behinds 10 metres in front of them. Down to the covered market of Saluhallen before we turn back again. We meet the same police officers who are now on their way down, and they are waiting for us. But we are quick and they are heavy. I am laughing so much that I get a stomach cramp. Johan is more tired, his face is red and his running is getting a bit laboured. He looks slightly panicked.

The police are gaining on us, and I get a flashback to the time at school when the older boys were chasing me. Now it feels more real.

'Come on now, Johan. We have to get a shift on.'

We've got a lead of 40 metres and we run between some houses, where we hide behind some bushes. The police lose sight of us.

'Where did those idiots go?' I hear one of them say quite close to us. 'They will get a slap where it hurts if I catch up with them.'

We stay absolutely silent, our hands covering our mouths to stifle our giggles.

Finally they move off.

My head feels good. The grinding has stopped. I've been laughing and running and I've been chased by the police.

THE EUROPEAN JUNIOR CHAMPIONSHIPS are getting closer. My coach is hoping that I will qualify. I just have to move up a notch. I have to get it together.

We are sitting with two other runners in a Volvo 740 on our way to Austria. It is warm and the windows are down. We're going to the Alps for altitude training, to build up our red blood cells with the help of the thin air.

I'm not at all in the mood for this, I'd rather be at home on Öckerö. Just a few days earlier a few mates and I jumped from the Fotöbron – 20 metres down to the sea. I can still feel the butterflies from that jump.

My coach is gulping coffee from his thermos. We are driving fast, get right down into southern Germany on the first day, and we check into a hotel. I have never slept under such heavy covers before, 40 centimetres thick.

The following afternoon we get to Austria, where we check into the hostel that will be our base for the next two weeks. It lies at 2000 metres. I've never been this high up before.

We change into our running gear at once and go off on our first training session. My body is heavy and unresponsive after sitting still for two days. My brain feels slow.

We do a distance run through the mountains at a moderate pace. The thin air makes me breathless and my heart beats faster. The high mountains are wherever I look. Cows grazing on the slopes. The contrast between the green grass and the snow-covered peaks. I've never seen anything like this before.

We work hard. There's a lot of intensive training mixed with gentle distance running in the mountains. It's fun, but I still feel worn out after the hard training during the winter. I realise that I have never really had time to recuperate.

When we get home there will be important races to run. They mean a lot and I want to get rid of whatever this problem is with my body. But my legs are heavy and they are constantly stinging.

When there are only a few days left of the camp, we are going to run 400-metre intervals downhill. With the help of the slope we are going to do some speed training. I will run 10 intervals. I am good at running downhill. I can run fast and have no fear of falling. My legs move with the speed of drumsticks.

After six intervals my right instep collapses and my foot goes flat. It's incredibly painful. There's a stabbing, burning, cutting pain with every step. I can't put any weight on the foot.

I go to lie down in my room. The foot swells up and I feel the pulse pounding across the top of my foot.

After a while my coach comes in to ask how I'm doing. I tell him what's happening and that it really hurts and that there's this pounding in my foot.

'It will be difficult to run tomorrow,' I say.

My coach tells me to keep the foot elevated and that will reduce the swelling, and as he goes out he says, 'Tomorrow we'll be doing intervals on the track.'

I SLEEP WITH MY FOOT ELEVATED all night. When I put my foot on the floor in the morning, the swelling comes back at once and the pins and needles are agonising. I can't walk without limping.

We have breakfast: hot chocolate and white bread with cheese. We take the car down to the track where we're going to do our interval training. It's warm and the track smells of rubber.

We sit down in the stands and the coach gives his instructions: 'You are going to do staggered training: 1000 metres, 800 metres, 600 metres, 400 metres and 200 metres. Two minutes' rest after each one. Markus, you've got to run the first thousand fast, preferably below 2 minutes 40. Then we'll see what happens.'

I limp off to warm up with the others. I try and jog as gently as I can, but my foot is just stinging and pounding. It hurts, both when I land on it and when I push off. We jog for four kilometres.

After the warm-up, I walk up to the coach and say that I can't run intervals today, that my foot is hurting too much. He looks at me for a moment without saying anything. Then he says: 'Markus, it's all in your head.'

'But look at my foot,' I say. 'It's swollen.'

'I don't want to look at your foot, there's nothing wrong with it. The problem is in your head.'

'But I can hardly jog, how am I going to manage running intervals?'

'Markus, for God's sake, get real! You're going to do the intervals, full stop.'

He kicks a pair of running shoes lying on the stand, screaming and shouting. He picks up my water bottle and throws it across the stand. The top flies off and the water runs out.

'Time to put on your spikes now! Stop whingeing.'

I'm 1000 miles from home and I just want to lie next to Mum on the sofa.

None of my training mates says anything. Everything is quiet.

I am wondering if I will be allowed to go home in the car with them. The fear makes my face go stiff, I can feel it around my mouth. I want to cry, but I don't. It's as if I have a pipe in my chest that carries all my feelings down to my stomach, where they end up in a heap.

I love running and pushing myself until my legs and lungs hurt. That's when I feel alive and in the moment. That's the way I want to live my life.

But not any more.

I put on my spikes and run the first interval in 2 minutes 38 seconds. I cut out the pain, I don't feel it.

I sit silently in the back seat all the way home. No one says anything to me. It's as if I don't exist.

I get to Lilla Varholmen's ferry station late at night after a thousand silent miles in the car. I take a deep breath as I recognise the warm, salty smell. I look at the sea and the boats.

I walk the final few kilometres from the ferry with my rucksack on my back. The house is silent when I get back home. Mum and Dad are asleep.

MUM IS SITTING ON the toilet. She needs help to wipe herself. I attach the harness around her stomach and lift her up.

I have done this God knows how many times, but it still feels strange to help her with this. I put a nappy in her pants and pull up her trousers.

Mum gives me a look that says: 'How strange that I am hanging here like this and you are pulling up my knickers.'

I lie her down on her sofa with a pillow under her legs. She wants a blanket over her.

'Turn on the CD player, I want to listen to Carola. Her Christmas disc.'

My foot is totally fucked. I can't run a metre. I've got no way to let off steam any more.

My chest feels fit to burst, as if my whole body wants to leak out on to the ground, to be absorbed into the soil and disappear.

I'm angry and I think I've had enough of it all.

The doctor at the clinic says that it's going to take a long time for my foot to get better. Every morning I tape up my instep with heavy-duty tape so that I can at least walk without it hurting.

I get up at 5.00 in the morning to prepare wholemeal porridge, which I have soaked overnight. I chew each mouthful 150 times. It takes me an hour to eat a bowl of porridge. My tongue gets chafed and cracked and smells odd.

In the day I shovel seaweed and in the evenings I work with Mum.

JOHAN AND I ARE SITTING in the backseat of a car on the way to Landvetter's church. Johan's dad is driving. We're smartly dressed, black trousers and white shirts. I've borrowed a pair of black shoes from a relative.

I'm one of the pallbearers.

My mate was 19 and I talked to him the day before it happened. He was one of Sweden's best kickboxers. He was 1.9 metres tall and weighed 90 kilos. Big, calm and cheerful, my absolute opposite. His nose was crooked, and his hair cropped.

He was going rock-climbing in northern Norway. He was alone and it was a couple of kilometres from the house where he was staying. The rock wasn't that high and there hadn't been any rockfalls there since the Second World War.

He was sitting at the foot of the cliff when a boulder was dislodged. It was big and heavy and tore off his leg at the thigh.

He had a climbing harness, which he tried to tie as tightly as possible to stop the blood that was pumping out of his leg. He crawled for 150 metres before he bled out.

I wonder what was going through his head. The panic and the loneliness. Feeling life draining out with every beat of his heart. Knowing that the very function of his heart was now bringing him death.

I am carrying the coffin on my left shoulder. It hurts, it's heavy.

No tears, just emptiness.

After the burial, Johan and I go out to the Hönö cliffs. We walk along the west side, and sit down right by the water's edge. We see the Vinga lighthouse way out there. The sea is shining and still.

We talk about how strange it is that one of our friends isn't alive any more. Quite suddenly the wind starts to blow, harder and harder. The rain comes, lashing our faces. The waves are foaming, and the wind gets stronger all the time.

Then all of a sudden it's quiet again. As if nothing had happened.

'What was that?' I say.

'I think that the Boxer has left us,' says Johan.

WITH THE AUTUMN come the storms. I put on swimming trunks, a thick sweater and a white knitted hat and cycle out to Hummer beach on the west side of Öckerö. It's now a storm-force wind, building up and getting stronger the closer it comes to land.

I walk over the rocks to get as far out into the bay as possible, and I put the sweater and hat out of the wind under a stone. The chill bites into my skin. The sea is foaming and looks like washing-up water. The strong wind pushes towards the shore birds that we never see on the islands, big sea birds that we usually see only out there on the distant horizon.

The waves arrive in threes – three big ones, and then it calms down a bit. I jump in after the third wave and swim under water and then dive under the biggest waves. There are a lot of jellyfish and the stings from them really hurt.

I swim against the waves and currents as long as I can.

When my muscles are cold and stiff and I don't have any strength left, I let the waves carry me back into the bay. It's hard to get back onto dry land, the waves are big and the rocks are slippery. I scrape my thighs against barnacles until they bleed. The salt stings in the cuts.

Johan and I go down to the shipyard in the port. It's late at night and pitch-black. We climb the fence around it. Everything is silent. Big, dark ships with gleaming propellers are laid up in the dry dock. I have always been terrified of propellers, imagining that one day I might be run over by a fishing boat while I am out for one of my long swims. The propeller would chop me up into pieces.

I can feel the adrenaline as a feather-light pressure below my breastbone, pushing my breath upwards. We run over to the big crane and begin climbing.

No lights come on. Higher and higher. We climb up as far as we can. We see the ground and the sea 25 metres below us.

My palms start to get sweaty, I can feel the crane moving in the wind. We climb out along the arm that sticks straight out from the wheelhouse. I go first and Johan follows.

The arm is swaying. The iron beams are strong, but I am still worried whether they will hold.

When we have got right to the end, I hang upside down from my knees over the precipice. I see the port and the boats upside down.

Up here life is simple. The only thing I need to do is to keep hanging on.

MUM IS SITTING IN HER electric wheelchair. I've secured her with the seat belt. Today she's cheerful and her hands aren't shaking all that much.

Outside, the autumn winds are blowing; there are no colours, only grey.

We go down the hill from the house and right away my hands are freezing and I have to run back to the house to get my gloves.

'Wait here. Don't go anywhere!' I tell her.

I'm back a couple of minutes later and she's just gone. Shit, she's such hard work!

I go down to the store. She isn't there. Bloody hell!

I get Grandad's bike. Where has she gone? She loves the sea and the port. I cycle towards the port, peddling hard. She'll be for it when I find her.

I get to the port, but she's nowhere to be seen. Can she have fallen in? She loves going near the edge. I look down in the water but I can't see anything.

I ride home a different way, but still no sign of Mum. I get back home and lean the bike against a wall.

I try a different approach and scream: 'MUUUUMMM.' No response.

I look into the garden of Öckerö's most eccentric old woman and under an apple tree I see Mum sitting there, bent forward like one of those curved yellow cheese puffs, stuck fast below a branch. I pull her free.

She doesn't say anything, looking up at me with eyes that seem to say: 'Markus, look at these apples. They're great. I had to take one. I just felt the urge.'

WE ARE SITTING IN MUM's car, a red Renault Kangoo. Mum has a special seat that makes it easier for me to lift her into the car.

We are going to an evangelical meeting at Hisingen, where a South African preacher with healing powers is going to speak.

I don't feel like going, I don't want to stand next to Mum and feel all those sympathetic looks. I've been there so many times before.

We arrive late and find seats in the back row. Mum is sitting in her wheelchair in the aisle.

The preacher begins: 'It's wonderful to be here in Hisingen. I think that God is with us tonight. Open your hearts and let in the power of the Holy Spirit. I had a fantastic meeting yesterday. People were healed. They threw away their crutches and started dancing. They could see again. There were tears of joy. Seventeen of them accepted the faith and allowed the Lord of Light into their lives. Christianity is growing in the world. Amen.'

Mum is hopeful, she says it's time for her to get well again.

'There are some people here who I would like to come forward,' says the preacher. 'I want to pray for you to be healed. With God's help I want to make you well.'

'HALLELUJAH,' says the congregation.

'There is a woman who has impure thoughts, and an old man who has problems with his legs. A woman who has a muscular condition. You can all come forward.'

Mum gives me a pleading look.

'I want to go up there,' she says. 'He's speaking to me. I've bought a pair of roller skates. They're in my cupboard at home.'

'What?'

'I'll use them when I'm well again.'

There is not a shadow of doubt in her eyes.

'OK,' I say.

The preacher starts with the old man. He lays a hand on his head and raises the other towards heaven. The people in the front rows stand up, their eyes closed and their arms raised to heaven.

'I pray in the name of Jesus,' the preacher intones. 'Throw away your crutches. Start walking!'

The man takes a few stumbling steps.

'Have faith that this healing will last. God listens to your prayers. Go in peace. Thank you, Jesus.'

The preacher goes up to Mum. He holds her head between his hands and starts praying in a loud voice. Finally he stops and says: 'Stand up!'

Mum shakes her head and looks at me.

'I can't. My legs are the same as ever,' she mumbles.

I tell the preacher that Mum hasn't stood up for years.

'It doesn't matter, you must dare to believe. Trust in the power of the Holy Spirit.'

He calls for two helpers who take hold of Mum under her arms and try to lift her up, but her legs just hang down and they can't do it. They put her back down in the wheelchair.

The preacher calls for another two helpers. Now Mum stands up, held there by four people. Her body is shaking, her head is hanging down.

'Take a step in faith. Trust that it will work.'

Mum tries. Nothing happens.

They put her back in her wheelchair.

'You just have to have more faith,' says the preacher and moves on to the woman with the impure thoughts.

I push Mum back to the back of the hall. It feels like everyone is staring at us.

'I don't understand anything,' says Mum. 'It does say: "Pray and you shall be given."'

'I know,' I say.

After the meeting we go down to the seafront. The wind is blowing.

I am frustrated, tired of all the shallow preachers and their big words. Mum has already let it go.

We eat sweets and watch the sun set over the sea.

MY FOOT IS STILL SWOLLEN. I really can't run.

I've got to get away. Away from Öckerö, away from tears and nagging and arguments about wet towels.

When two of my mates tell me that they are going to India, I decide to go along with them. We are going to be there for 10 weeks, just travelling around, checking out the Himalayas. After my summer job on the beaches I have some money saved and my back is still tanned.

We take the boat to England, where we are going to be flying from Heathrow. On the way there things go wrong and we just about catch the plane, but our luggage doesn't.

WHEN WE LAND IN DELHI, we have only the clothes we're wearing: jeans and thick sweaters. It's 37°C. We check into a youth hostel and head out into the city looking for some lighter clothes.

I'm sweaty and feel like a giant. Everyone around us is tiny and thin. Everyone seems to come up so close to us.

We decide to go on to Nepal as soon as we get our rucksacks.

THE BUS TO KATHMANDU is full of people and chickens. The journey should take 12 hours.

A wrinkled old woman is sitting next to me. She chats on and on, and I don't understand a thing, but that doesn't seem to matter. The chickens cluck and the people fart and belch.

Everything smells a lot – smells that are unfamiliar.

After 24 hours we are halfway there. I am hungry and desperate for a pee and I don't want to sit still any longer. The woman next to me is using my shoulder as a pillow.

All of a sudden the bus stops. The driver stands up and announces loudly: 'It's a bus strike. You've all got to get off. It usually only lasts a couple of days.'

We check into a hostel nearby. It's nice to strip down to my pants and stretch out on the bed, under a refreshing fan. My mates go out to get some hash.

They come back in a little while with narrow pupils and an intense craving for sweets. I keep away from all that because I'm conscious of my tendency to take everything too far. There's no point in opening that particular door.

After three days the strike is over and we head off, this time better prepared with more water and more fruit. After a few hours, the bus stops for a toilet break.

I find it hard to get the stream started, but at last my prostate relaxes and all is well. Just when I am in full flow, the bus starts to head off.

I stem the flow and pull up my pants as fast as I can and limp after the bus, which accelerates with a black cloud belching out of the exhaust. I haven't got a chance of catching up.

My friends are sitting asleep on the bus. One of them has my wallet. My thoughts are whirring in my skull – it doesn't seem to be a great idea to be left out here without a penny to my name.

About 100 metres further on, the bus brakes to let a water buffalo cross.

I run as fast as I can. There's a screaming pain in my foot, and when I am five metres away from the bus it starts to accelerate off again, but this time I manage to grab hold of the ladder that hangs down over the rear window.

I pull myself up and sit down on the roof. I let out a huge sigh of relief. I lie down and look up at the sky, and let the warm air blow over me. I continue the journey up there.

AFTER A FEW DAYS IN KATHMANDU, we carry on through the mountains up to Jiri, the point of departure for our trek to Mount Everest. It will take us a month there and back.

In the hostel we eat fried rice and vegetables. I decide that I don't need to eat too much because I can't run.

We start off our walk with a seriously steep uphill section that makes our legs sting. It's warm and clammy. We walk through a damp forest on dirt tracks full of leeches that bite us without us noticing. My blood is as thin as water as it runs down my calves.

It's easy to find bed and board along the way, so we travel light with our sleeping bags and some spare clothes. In the day I eat crackers with peanut butter, and in the evenings we stuff ourselves with whatever they serve at the hostels – most often fried rice, sometimes with yak-milk cheese. A cup of tea with sugar for afters. There are bedbugs in the beds and our bodies never stop itching.

The further up the mountains we get, the colder it is. The air is thinner and we can feel this in our heads. In the night, the temperature falls below zero and the stars feel very close.

I love using my legs as a means of transport. It's not fast, but you have the time to see everything around you. To experience all the smells and the colours.

After two weeks we reach Kala Patthar, where you have a view of Everest. We get up early and walk up the hill to look at the world at sunrise.

It's -15°C and there's no wind. In the morning we take off our clothes and stand naked in the cold with our faces towards the mountain. It doesn't look all that high.

We go on to base camp, which lies a few hours further along the valley at an altitude of 5500 metres. I jog for a bit to see how the foot feels. Better, but not good. Still, it's nice to be able to move my legs a bit faster.

The base camp is crammed with colourful tents and climbers who are going to try to make it to the summit. The big ice sheet that constitutes the door to Everest is just a stone's throw away.

The last time that the Boxer and I talked, we spoke about Everest and trying to get there one day. Now here I am, but without him.

WE START THE JOURNEY BACK. The air becomes less thin the further down we get. More power in each breath.

One week away from Jiri, I start to run a temperature and begin coughing. My body feels weird, lacking in energy. We shorten our daily distances, but it doesn't help. My temperature rises and my cough is getting worse.

My friends find a field of wild cannabis. They pick and pick, using the raincover for the rucksacks as a container. When we get to the hostel at night, they spread out the weed on the beds to dry it off a bit.

In Jiri they pack the cannabis into little parcels, which they post without a sender's name to different friends in Sweden. Foolproof.

Back in Kathmandu I go straight to the hospital. When I get in to see the doctor, he is busy carrying out heart massage on a bleeding man who is lying on a gurney behind the desk. I sit down on a chair and look on.

The doctor carries on the procedure for another minute or so before giving up. He turns to face me: 'So, what's the matter with you then?'

'A pain in my chest and a temperature. And my farts smell of eggs.'

I can't take my eyes off the dead man in the background.

'Nothing I could do,' says the doctor nodding towards him. 'A car accident.'

He listens to my chest and takes my pulse.

'You've got pneumonia,' he says. 'I'll give you a prescription for antibiotics. Those eggy farts are down to an amoeba in your stomach. I'll give you a pill for that as well.'

WHEN I GET BACK HOME FROM INDIA, it's November and dark and cold outside. I have lost eight kilos. The cough is still there.

Mum is lying on the sofa when I walk through the door. She welcomes me with a tired smile. I lie down next to her and tell her about the trip.

Grandad is preparing a fish that is bubbling away on the cooker and I fill my stomach with protein from the sea.

I fill up the bath with warm water and lie there until my skin is all wrinkled, and wash away the flea bites and the smells from India.

After just two weeks, things start to överwhelm me again. The panic, the stress.

My foot is still not up to any running. Mum lies weeping on the sofa, when she isn't nagging me about the curtains. Grandma keeps on at me, saying that I am now a grown-up and must start supporting myself.

'You can't stay here at home just using other people,' she says. 'You have to move out. Mum doesn't want you here.'

I am walking around on tiptoes, trying to melt into the background like a piece of furniture.

It feels like I'm carrying a heavy weight around in my body and I can barely walk. I am finding it difficult to sleep. I am completely obsessed with the idea that I am sick like Mum. Now it's starting, now it's all downhill. Soon I will be there with my head hanging down, never running again, never swimming. Just lying on the sofa listening to Carola.

I go to the neurology department in Gothenburg for some tests. The doctor does his stuff, he tests my reflexes and balance. I stand on one leg with my eyes closed.

'It all looks fine,' he says. 'We can test your spinal fluid as well, but there is a bit of a risk with that and it doesn't always tell you anything useful. I think you are healthy. If you have a parent with MS, there is only a two to three per cent risk that you will get it too.'

I feel slightly relieved.

MUM IS DRINKING HER COFFEE through a straw. She is sitting in her wheelchair at the white kitchen table. Her head moves from side to side and between the swallows I have to put the straw back into her mouth. She drinks a mouthful and it goes down the wrong way.

This often happens to Mum; the fluid wants to go down her airways instead of her oesophagus. She gets red in the face and looks really funny.

I slap her back, she coughs and the coffee comes up again. It's still a bit difficult for her to breathe.

'Come on, you chicken,' I say. 'Take a deep breath.'

Mum breathes and starts laughing. She laughs until her face is beetroot red.

'Mum, you look really weird. I mean, seriously ugly,' I say.

This makes her laugh even more hysterically. She can't stop and neither can I.

It's like a suppressed need, which just has to come up to the surface right now. Like a window to something else, something easier.

I go down to the store to pick up a few things. I am standing there trying to decide which kind of muesli we want, there are so many different ones. The whole shelf is full and I can't make up my mind. Instead I come back empty-handed.

When get back home, Mum wants to get up from the sofa.

I don't want to help her just at that point. I just can't manage it. I want to be left alone. I feel completely empty.

Mum starts to cry just as Grandad walks in the door, and she tells him that I don't want to help her. Grandad is furious: 'You godforsaken shit, you can't be serious! You are so spoiled. Your mum is lying there and can't do anything and you don't want to help her.'

I can feel an anger and a rage that I have never experienced before, a power that is frightening and beyond my control. I go up to Grandad and lift him up – he weighs 100 kilos, but in my arms he feels as light as straw – and throw him out through the door.

He falls on his front and scrapes his hands. He looks terrified. He's shaking.

'If you come back, I'll hit you properly,' I say and slam the door shut.

The tears are running down Mum's cheeks.

'You shut up,' I say. 'No more whingeing.'

ULF EKMAN, HEAD OF THE EVANGELICAL GROUP LIVETS ORD, is in town and Mum and I are going into Lundby for an evening meeting. We get there early. Mum wants to sit right at the front.

My body starts itching as we enter the hall. I really don't want to be here. I've grown tired of all the words, all those raised hands and loud prayers. But I am working with Mum and she's the one who decides.

We sit down at the front. I'm on a seat and Mum's next to me in her wheelchair. Mum says: 'I know what's the matter. He's deaf. He can't hear.'

'Who are you talking about?'

'God, of course. He doesn't hear what I am saying. If he can hear, then why am I sitting here?'

'Hard to know,' I say. 'Perhaps he has an odd sense of humour.'

After a while, the supporting preacher comes up to us and tells us to move.

'Why?' I ask.

'You can disturb the Holy Spirit if you stay there. You have to move further back.'

I just want to punch him really hard in the stomach. Mum says OK and we move.

MY SALVATION IS THE HÅLLAND FOLKHÖGSKOLA, the municipal adult education college in Jämtland. There they don't worry about my not having any qualifications from high school. I am studying to become a youth recreation leader concentrating on mountain sports and healthcare.

I share a flat with two classmates in the house of U-G, the headteacher. I spend my days at school, and I'm left to my own devices in the evenings – sprouting beans and playing ice hockey with the local team. I'm still good on skates, but my feel for the game has gone.

Hålland lies between the small communities of Järpen and Undersåker in the Åre municipality. The E14 runs along the foot of the hill with long-distance trucks going between Östersund and Trondheim. Right down in the valley flows the Indalsälven. In the distance you can see the mighty Ristafallet, which you can read about in Astrid Lindgren's *Ronja Rövardotter*.

Everyone knows everyone else in the village and the older people are curious in a nice way; they don't mind whether your hair is long or short.

I start to breathe again. To see the colours more clearly every moment I spend outside, to adjust to the clear air. The anxiety starts to evaporate.

My foot is getting a bit better every day and soon I can run again. My fitness is shot, but it is wonderful to feel my heart pumping. I run in the woods above the college over soft terrain, across marshes and cold streams. I see the mountains in the distance. I run on my own. I feel life and my strength returning.

I feel stronger the further I run, where nobody knows where I am.

In the college sauna I meet Kenth, a man from the village. He sits on the top bench. His face is red and the sweat is dripping off him. It's a super-hot sauna. I like him at once. One day Kenth tells me about a man who moved out into the woods. It may have been 20 years ago, the details are a little hazy. He settled somewhere along the Slagsån a bit further up the mountain, but exactly where and why no one remembers.

Every week U-G and I get caught up in some sort of discussion. We're either in his study at the college or just on the stairs at home. He's got long hair and is shorter than me, but he's scarily strong. His nails are cracked; it's unclear why, but I suspect that he's been out in the cold too much.

He asks me questions and awakens thoughts that have never occurred to me before. U-G has been a teacher for many years, teaching about the outdoor life, nutrition and training. He's in total control, but he never tells me what to do. We talk a lot about running.

'Markus, you have to become your own coach if you want to carry on running. Nobody else can know your body better than you do yourself. Running can be about becoming a greater human being, to find something beyond achievement and results. If you want to go on developing, don't look at it in a one-dimensional way.'

Every time we meet, he inspires me with new thoughts and ideas.

ONE DAY I PUT ON MY RUNNING SHOES and run along the path that goes from school over the hill up towards Helgesjön. After a few kilometres I reach the lake and follow the Slagsån downstream.

The river's edge is soggy and covered in shrubs and it's hard to get a clear run, so I take a path a bit further into the forest. It's drier at once and there are more fir trees. I run along, dipping under the branches, shielding my eyes.

A few kilometres further on, I get to a high ridge sloping steeply down to the river. I follow it and come to a bend in the ridge. Below it there's a grassy clearing.

This must be where he lived, that man who moved out into the forest. What a place.

I lie on my back in the grass. Eyes closed.

No wind, completely still.

The valley stretches in a west-east direction. On one side, the fir trees are tall and dense, protecting against the wind and providing dry branches for a fire. On the other side, the forest slopes down towards the river, giving a permanent supply of fresh, cold drinking water. Perfect.

It just seems completely obvious: this is where I am going to live after the summer.

No hesitation, just a deep sense of calm.

THE WOODS

On 6 August 1999, I get out of the train at Järpen. It's 7.30 in the morning, and I have travelled the whole night from Gothenburg. My back is stiff, I have been sitting up all night

I start to make my way towards Helgesjön. My rucksack is heavy, packed with 40 kilos of clothes, equipment and food. I have tied the sleeping mat and the sleeping bag on the steel frame under the bag. The axe, saw and knife are secured on the outside.

The food I've brought can't go bad. I've focused on things that last: cereal grains, nuts, lentils and crispbread; raisins, prunes and additive-free dried apricots; carrots and onions; butter, salt, cinnamon and black pepper. I'm planning to harvest vitamin C from the forest for as long as possible: lady's mantle, wild raspberries and lingon. And cloudberries, the gold of the mountains.

I walk around in hiking trousers and a thin woollen sweater, with heavy boots on my feet. They are new and stiff and I am wearing double socks to avoid blisters.

In my rucksack I've got my running clothes and shoes, lightweight sandals, Mum's white raincoat, a thick knitted sweater, hat and gloves, two pairs of woollen long johns and underwear, and three pairs of thick socks that Grandma has knitted for me from hard-wearing wool.

The plan is just to use cotton and wool. Wool will wash itself if I hang it from a branch in the woods on a rainy day. It never smells bad and doesn't burn easily. Cotton is soft and gentle, it feels nice against the skin. It is also good at keeping out sparks from the fire.

I might have to buy more clothes when winter comes, but I am counting on managing like this for a good long while.

IT TAKES ME THREE HOURS to get to the clearing. I take off my rucksack and lie down on my front, stretching out my back.

The grass is still bright green. The sound from the Slagsån is less audible than in the spring, not as intense.

This is where I am going to live. I have no idea how it's going to work out or what I have embarked on. I only know that this is what I want to do.

I have decided to live outdoors for at least a year, through all the seasons. I want to see how the forest and nature will affect me.

I chop down 15 slim fir trees and strip the bark off. They will provide the frame of my kåta, a traditional Saami tent. My hands are covered with a resin that is sticky and smells good. My fingers stick together; the axe is glued to my hand.

I tie three of the fir poles together with strong cord to form a tripod, against which I lean the rest of the poles. It takes me the whole day to erect the complete frame.

When it starts to get dark, I take off my clothes and go down to have a wash in the river. My skin feels rough in the cool night, and the mosquitoes are biting. I use the axe to scrape the resin off my hands and then I jump into the water, washing under my arms with soap. My willy shrinks to a raisin in the cold water. I haven't got a towel, so I dry myself with my hands and shake the water from my hair.

When I am dressed again I light a fire and make some porridge. After a whole day without food it is wonderful to fill the empty hole in my stomach with oatmeal and carrots.

I gather together some branches beneath a huge fir, get out the sleeping mat and the sleeping bag and crawl inside. The rucksack is my pillow.

It smells of pine and fire. All is still.

I don't want to be anywhere else.

I AM WOKEN UP BY the itching and stinging. I am lying face down in the fir branches and the mosquitoes have feasted on my blood. I am rested, but my body feels strangely out of shape after the night's sleep.

It's all happening in the forest: the birds are singing and the mosquitoes are staying out of the sun. I walk down to the river for a drink, eat two carrots and put on my running shoes. I run the five kilometres down to the E14 to meet a guy who's selling me the canvas cover for my tent. It's been stitched together from closely woven, waterproof cotton and has an opening at the front. Once, I saw an old man selling hot dogs from this kind of tent in Åre and was told that it was a ready-made model called the Moskosel Kåta. Now the man by the side of the road has 1700 kronor [$200] in his hand and the tent cover is mine.

Back in the clearing I unfold the light-coloured material and drape it around the frame. I make sure that the opening faces east so that the morning sun will provide light and warmth when I get up, and I secure the cover with sharpened tent pegs that I hammer into the ground with the back of the axe.

Down at the river I look for the right size stones for the fireplace, which I am building in the middle of the tent, right below the smoke vent. Between some poles I put up washing lines to hang up my clothes and sleeping bag, and I prepare some bedding from the fir branches at the back of the tent so that I can watch the opening from where I sleep. I light a fire and make myself a soup from lentils and stock, add some olive oil and eat until my stomach tells me to stop.

I can feel the rain in the air as I pull on my shorts and running shoes. I run off and find an animal path, which I follow until the strength in my legs is starting to give out. I come back home soaked to the skin as darkness falls.

I feel comfortable as my body winds down. I light a fire in the fireplace. The dry fir branches spit out sparks with a crackling noise.

I boil some water with a few raisins, add 200ml of oats and make a sweet porridge. I top this off with a handful of nuts and eat it straight out of the saucepan with a wooden spoon, which I made in woodwork when I was very young. I take out my sleeping mat and turn on my side to look at the fire.

Back at home I am sure that Mum has already gone to bed. Grandad may be on his way out to the lake to set his nets.

I let the fire burn itself out before I go down to the river to brush my teeth. I put some cold water into the porridge saucepan.

Back at the tent I say my normal evening prayer, 'Gud som haver' ['God, who holds the children dear'], and fall asleep to the sound of rain falling on the canvas.

I HAVE TO FIX A PROPER BED. It's not really working out sleeping on prickly branches. Also the ground isn't quite even, so my back still feels out of shape every time I wake up.

I run off to the Hållandsgården, our local hotel and conference centre next to the college, and ask the manager if they have an old bed that they want to get rid of. He gives me one that they were going to throw out.

The wooden frame is heavy and awkward as I drag it on my back through the forest, and I get terrible blisters on my shoulder blades. It takes me hours to get back. In the tent I construct a support for the bed frame from some rocks and use a transparent bottle of water as a spirit level to make sure it's absolutely right. I put down the sleeping mat and a reindeer skin, lie down on the bed and fall asleep straight away.

I wake up hungry and thirsty a few hours later. I make soup and tea from some lady's mantle. It doesn't taste too good, but I have heard that it's good for you. I run back through the woods to Hållandsgården to pick up the horsehair mattress that they also gave me. It's easier to carry, doesn't chafe against my back as much.

So now I have a bed and a fairly soft mattress. It has taken me all day, and it's wonderful.

THE NEXT DAY I SAW down some dry fir trees near the tent. The trees are dead and will burn well, and they also don't have any sticky resin.

I chop off all the dry branches and saw the trunks into three-metre lengths, which I drag through the woods, my legs bent and my back straight. It's heavy work, but it feels good. I feel strong.

Back at the tent I cut down the trunks into 30-centimetre sections, which I split for firewood on my woodblock. It takes time; each trunk takes a whole day. When my arms and shoulders are gone, I run one circuit. I'll get the reward for all my work when winter comes, and my supply should last until spring.

Days pass. I saw, chop, run, make fires, eat and sleep.

After two weeks, half the tent is taken up with five cubic metres of firewood. I lean the other dry firs against a tree nearby so that they won't become soaked and rotten with the autumn rains.

The food is starting to run out and I walk around with an empty feeling in my stomach, and my brain seems to work more and more slowly. I put on my rucksack and run along an access road for forestry workers around Norsjön towards Järpen and the nearest foodstore.

It isn't very comfortable to run with my rucksack, it's much too big. It takes me an hour to cover the 10 kilometres.

When I arrive I take out 300 kronor [$35] from the cash machine. My plan is to live on less than 1000 kronor [$115] a month. Since porridge is my staple diet I convert everything into oatmeal. A pair of new running shoes costs 1000 kronor, or 150 kilos of oats for the same money.

As I enter the shop I realise I smell of smoke. I hadn't noticed this earlier. I buy oatmeal, nuts, salt, lentils, vegetables, butter and fruit, and a bar of chocolate that I will have on Saturday.

I am eating a piece of fruit and a few nuts as I wander homewards. I get back three hours later with enough food to last two weeks. I fix a rich soup with butter and green lentils. I can feel my blood carrying the nourishment to my muscles. Everything feels perfect.

I lay my sleeping bag on the grass outside the tent and settle down. I look up at the sky.

I WAKE UP WITH A FEELING of restlessness in my body. It jerks and itches.

Everything has been done – the firewood is stacked and the bed is fixed, I've had enough to eat and my storage box is full. I've nothing left to do.

Before I moved out here, this is what I wanted to achieve. I just wanted to be inside my own head.

Now I've got there and I'm starting to sense some kind of resistance.

What am I doing here? This is such bloody hard work.

My head is full of new thoughts.

I lay down on my bed, watching the sky through the smoke vent. I do nothing.

When it starts to get dark a few hours later, things feel easier. I go out into the autumn dusk and I take the path that goes parallel with the river to collect birch bark. After a while, I feel that I am being watched and I turn around quickly. Is there someone standing behind a tree over there?

Good God, who can it be? Panic. I close my eyes tight, and then look over there again. I don't see anything this time either.

What's going on? Am I starting to see things? Perhaps I'm going insane?

I rush back to the tent and light a fire, all the time facing the opening. I want to have a good view. I expect someone to open it and step inside.

I don't have any supper. I just crawl into my sleeping bag and fall asleep with my back against the canvas and my eyes towards the opening of the tent.

I WALK THROUGH THE FOREST. The air feels icy and damp and the sky is dark with heavy clouds. I'm wearing Mum's white raincoat and I'm walking fast. I hear a branch snapping behind me and I prick up my ears as I turn round.

I see nothing. I hear nothing.

Perhaps it was just an elk?

Perhaps it was something else?

The adrenaline is pumping, I can't walk any longer. I start running, I can't resist the impulse, I'm just reacting. I accelerate until I am running as fast as I possibly can. It doesn't help, I am getting more and more frightened. Jesus, please help me!

I tear off the white raincoat. I don't want to be visible in the dark. I roll it up and push it under my sweater. I hide under a fir tree where I crouch down, waiting. I am quite still.

Nothing happens.

It feels safe to be leaning against the tree. I stay put.

After what seems like an eternity, I crawl from my hiding place and start walking home. It's tough to leave the tree.

I RUN ROUND Norsjön towards Helgesjön, see the Åreskutan mountain 15 kilometres to the west, tripping through marshes and wading across tiny streams. The air is cold and I am wearing a thin woolly top and a pair of blue tights that I was given by that shouting trainer of mine. I am wet up to my knees, my hands are cold, but my body is kept warm by all this exercise.

I haven't seen another human being in three weeks. I am talking loudly to myself and sing songs so that I can at least hear my own voice.

I have never spent so much time on my own. It feels strange. Time moves more slowly. I breathe more deeply, and I can feel my heart beating.

The sun is high in the sky and everything is actually quite simple. I'm not freezing. I'm not hungry. The mosquitoes are gone, I'm no longer itching, but I have no peace. I have nothing to do.

I see a birch and suddenly have the urge to climb it. I heave myself up on to a branch and climb higher and higher, branch after branch until I can't go any further. I stop with my foot lodged in the fork of a branch.

The tree sways in the wind. I look out across the valley. I see the shifting colours of the fir trees. I close my eyes and disappear into myself.

I don't read any books here. I don't listen to the radio. I don't watch the TV. I don't feed on other people's opinions, don't have to fit into any other context.

I can't bear being with people; everyone keeps on talking, too many words and opinions that aren't based on anything. Everything is surface, no depth. So many answers, endless debates on television, I wish that everyone would just shut up.

I can't find any direction in the ordinary plastic existence, I think everything seems a waste of time – I don't want to have to choose between different kinds of shit, I want to choose between good and bad, or good and evil, between life and death.

I want my choices to have consequences – if I make the wrong choice, it should really hurt.

Am I running away from something?

I stand there until my foot starts hurting.

When I get back home again, I have run 25 kilometres, my legs feel weak. I take off my wet clothes and hang them on the line, tie the shoelaces together and hang up the shoes. They smell of marsh and earth.

IT'S THE AFTERNOON. The sun is tired, but the light is warm, and I run from the Slagsån up to the marsh below the heights of Romohöjden. On the top of Åreskutan the snow is sticking. I run across the marsh and my legs feel light.

I run in giant strides across the mountain slopes, all the way down to the river Indalsälven and past the Ristafallet waterfall. I continue down the path along the river and get back on the hill, three kilometres of steep uphill running. I move effortlessly and come back to the marsh with the sun on my back.

Then I hear the call of an elk. I stop. After a while, I hear another elk answering a bit further away. I put my thumb and index finger across my nose and make a call of my own and both elks answer.

They are both quite close and I stand still. At last they come out onto the marsh with 30 metres between them. I don't move. Nor do the elks, and their big ears are pointing towards me like satellite dishes. We form a triangle – the bull, the cow and I. The elks have got the evening sun in their eyes and the wind at their backs. Their legs are long and thin, and they look strong.

I run on, and so do the elks. There are crashing sounds from the forest as they disappear.

When I reach the lake Helgesjön I take off my clothes and jump in, and swim around until the mud and sweat has been washed away.

I rub my armpits with sand and walk naked through the forest all the way back home to the tent.

I put on my underclothes, my thick socks and hat. Steam comes from my mouth when I breathe out. I go out into the forest to collect birch bark and fine twigs to use as kindling. I split some logs for when the fire has taken. I build the fire up with bigger and bigger branches. I keep the fire going until it's warm inside the tent, and I warm away the dampness from the canvas.

The forest is silent. My face is warm from the fire. Outside there's a wall of darkness.

I eat crispbread with butter and drink some warm water, let the fire burn down and go to bed. I write down the events of the day in my diary. I watch the stars through the smoke vent.

I like lying there wrapped up in my sleeping bag, feeling the cold night air against my face.

SÖREN, A JOURNALIST WHO LIVES next door to the college, says one day that he wants to do a feature on me for the *Östersunds-Posten*, the local paper. We meet in Hålland and go out to the tent together.

We talk about the forest and about what is happening inside my head when it's quiet and about why I live here. I have no answers, I've lived outdoors for only a short time. I just know that I think that the forest can help me to find some direction.

The piece appears in the paper a few days later. I read it at the college, see myself in a colour photo spread across the centrefold, in a green sweater and a grey knitted hat.

When I meet Sören a few days later, he tells me he's sold the article on to *Aftonbladet* and *Göteborgs-Posten*. I don't get it, why this interest? I'm not doing anything.

Sometime later I'm told that someone has phoned from SVT, Sweden's national broadcaster. I get a number and call them back.

It's the sports department, who are wondering if they can come up and film a bit. After giving it some thought, I agree.

Micke Leijnegard and a cameraman come out to the tent and stay there for one night, spent on thin sleeping mats on the ground next to the woodpile. The next day they film me lighting fires and running and doing all the stuff that I've been doing the last few months. It becomes a five-minute item shown in the main sports programme one Sunday a few weeks later.

I sneak into the college and watch it with some of the students. It's fun, but again it feels a bit strange that I can be seen as interesting. After all, haven't there always been people living in the outdoors?

I MUST DO SOMETHING about my restlessness. One day I put on several layers of clothes, sit down on a tree stump and do nothing. I must get over this hurdle, I must learn how to do nothing.

I sit still, hour after hour.

I don't go inside until it's dark. I'm really tired although I haven't done anything. My brain feels completely wiped out.

I've a thousand ideas going round and round in my head. It's difficult to switch off when it's quiet, because then there's nothing to distract one's thoughts.

I make some buckwheat porridge with raisins, add some grated carrots and almond paste, and flavour it with cinnamon. I eat until I'm full and let the fire die down.

I go down to the stream wearing sandals. My toothpaste is finished, so I rub my teeth clean with a twig. I get cramp in my feet when I go into the ice-cold water. I dunk myself quickly and get back to the bank to soap myself. I rinse off the suds and then jog back up to the tent.

Still no towel, so I just brush off the water with my hands before putting on my warm underwear. I lie down on the bed and go straight to sleep. I sleep a dreamless sleep and wake up rested at the break of dawn the next day.

I'm feeling an awful pressure in my body. I want to cut down the whole forest. I want to exhaust myself working. I feel like the Incredible Hulk.

I lace up my boots and go up towards the top of the hill. I hold my breath for 50 steps and breathe for 20, all the way to the top. I am training myself to do without oxygen.

From the top I can see the spire of Undersåker church. Hear the train. See the Indalsälven. There's smoke rising from the water.

The sky is clear, the air is cold. My ears are wide open. I don't need to be selective. I take in every single sound.

I close my eyes and turn towards the sun. I sit there for a long, long time, resisting the impulse to go away. It is hard to just sit. It feels as if something is missing. Perhaps that's true. Perhaps I am missing something?

I force myself to stay.

THE HEAVENS OPEN, the rain is icy, almost snow. I am wet and cold, my hands are frozen stiff.

I've spent the day without any clear plan and I stop beneath a huge fir tree, where I take off my rucksack. I get out my thermos and some nuts and sit down on the rucksack, leaning against the tree. The branches keep the rain off me.

I eat a few peanuts and drink warm water with some mint leaves. It warms my stomach but doesn't reach my fingers. I try to warm my hands against my crotch and walk on. No sounds, the birds are quiet.

I get cold so easily, it's always been like that. When I was little, my lips were often blue and Mum was worried about my heart. 'Nothing wrong with his heart, just low blood pressure,' said the doctor.

When I get home to the tent it's dark and I catch the familiar smell of reindeer skin and smoke. I'm chilled to the bone, my lips feel cold and numb. I light the fire and get it going full blast. My hair dries, my lips thaw out, and my hands start to work again.

I take off my clothes and sit naked on the bed. I keep the fire going until I am warmed through.

I realise that winter will be my greatest challenge. I'm hoping that I will be able to cope with all of this, but I don't know.

IT IS NOVEMBER and it's pitch-black outside. I can't see my hand in front of my face when I walk through the forest. There are no stars in the sky, no snow yet to light up the world.

I am on edge. Someone is walking behind me.

I don't dare to use my torch. I don't want to be visible, nor do I want to know whatever it is that's behind me. I don't turn round, I don't walk faster, I've learned that such behaviour only makes it worse, that whatever is following will only come closer. I bend down and feel around for where the path leads, and I tiptoe slowly all the way home.

Back at the tent it feels as if someone is waiting for me there inside the darkness. I take a deep breath, close my eyes and go in. There's no one there.

I light the fire and sit down on the bed. My armpits stink of sweat, like some unwashed old man.

This isn't working any more. I'm so scared of the dark. I can't go on living out here if I feel like this.

I am trying to think rationally, but it's no bloody good.

I'm lying on my back, poking at the fire with a stick. The smoke is clear, the flames dancing up and down, the sparks are flying all over the place.

I pull a woollen blanket over my sleeping bag so that it doesn't get any more holes from the fire. It took quite a few mending sessions with the silver tape before that occurred to me. I fall asleep and am awoken by a hissing sound in my throat and it really hurts. I must have been sleeping with my mouth open, but still, what are the chances that a spark would find its way in there?

I get up and heat a little water, add some frozen honey and drink it in small gulps. The blister in my throat goes away.

I allow the fire to die down, pick up a reindeer skin and go to lie down outside.

I mustn't lose the battle against my fear of the dark.

IT'S COLD AND I HAVE already gone through the whole woodpile. I don't want to, but I have to go out into the darkness to collect something to make a fire.

I put on my cotton trousers and my thick winter boots. I have chopped down a fir tree, which is lying like a bridge across the Slagsån, and a bit further into the forest on the other side I've seen a few dead trees.

As I make may way cautiously across to the other side, the ghost pops up again. I stop and stand completely still. My fear washes over me. I can't hear anything. I carry on.

I tell myself that it isn't very likely that anyone is walking behind me. I know that it's just a phantom, a figment of my imagination, but that doesn't make any difference. I still feel it somewhere behind me.

I get to the dead trees, take down the smallest and chop off the dried branches. As I stand there, looking down at the ground, my back bent, the phantom sneaks up closer, but I decide to pretend not to notice.

I go back with the tree over my shoulder, it's heavy. Terror washes over me again. I stop. I close my eyes. I let it come. Bloody hell, won't it ever let go?

I'm consumed with rage and scream out across the darkness: 'Give up, will you? What do you want? You can leave me alone now and go and find someone else!'

I get to the tent and light the fire with birch bark and twigs, saw up the dry fir wood by the opening, still in a rage.

A LETTER ARRIVES FOR ME at the college from a documentary filmmaker called Peter Magnusson. He has read Sören's article in *Göteborgs-Posten* and asks if he can make a film about me. Peter is keen to know why I chose to live in the woods. What goes on in my head when it's all silent? What am I learning?

At first I think that it's too close to the bone, and that I won't cope. And I feel that television is the evil eye, a passive entertainment like overcooked porridge with too much sugar on top. There is also something disturbing about getting all this attention. After all, I want to live without things, to be cut off. I'm doing this for myself, not for anyone else. And have I actually got anything to say?

After pondering for a few days, I call Peter. He is 10 years older than me and grew up on Hisingen. Peter speaks in a really unrestrained, sweary Gothenburg dialect and used to play the drums in a punk band. He worked as a tiler before starting to make films.

He makes a good impression, he feels different. He's no snooty culture vulture. Peter explains what his plan is for the film: 'You just live your life and I will stand to the side with my camera like a tree in the forest. You won't do anything that you wouldn't do normally.'

I accept. I like to be alone, but if truth be known I also like to be noticed.

IT'S DECEMBER AND I HAVE been living outdoors for just over four months. Outside it's permanently below zero and the water itself is zero. I can still wash in the stream, but I have to make a fire first so that I am really warm when I go in.

I do this only every other day – and always while it's still light. When I wash myself, my hands and feet get incredibly cold, the veins contract and I can't move. On the way back to the tent, my hair turns to ice.

One evening the air feels different. Colder. Drier.

I go inside and lie down. I feel heavy, and long to sleep. I creep down into my sleeping bag and blow out the candle. I can't see anything through the smoke vent, no moon, no stars.

Inside the sleeping bag I feel safe; I like the feeling of being tightly wrapped up in soft material while my head is still out in the cold. I roll over onto my stomach and inhale the smell of the reindeer skins.

I wake at first light the next day. Something is different. The forest is completely silent.

I push aside the opening flap of the tent and go outside. Everything is white, covered in a soft white blanket. The snow has arrived.

I HAVE BEEN GIVEN A PAIR of cross-country skis by Bertil, who lives up in Duved. We met when I went to college. Bertil's son was the Norrland marathon champion and died when he was just 30, probably from TWAR, a kind of bacterial pneumonia. Bertil and I hit it off on a deep level right from the start. He sees me as I really am.

Now I need a pair of boots that fit my feet and thicker winter clothes. My legs are starting to get cold.

I go down to the E14 and hitch a lift all the way to Östersund. At the surplus store I find a pair of tough, old-fashioned trousers – a little too big, but they'll do. I buy two pairs of long johns and a pair of thick mittens. I'm 180 kronor [$20] poorer when I leave the store.

I change outside the store, decked out as it is in Christmas decorations, and stuff the thinner clothes into my rucksack. On my feet I've got leather boots with a woollen lining. It's -12°C, and icy, thin snow is falling.

By the last roundabout on the road towards Trondheim I wait on the roadside for five minutes before I am picked up by a heavy rocker. AC/DC and the Ramones are playing on the stereo. This isn't my style; I prefer instrumental music, wistful melodies that go straight into the heart.

In Järpen I jump out and go into the discount shop Kupan, where I find a pair of heavy size 43 boots for 15 kronor [$1.70]. They are a perfect fit. I put them in my rucksack and start out on the 10-kilometre walk home.

I have been on the go all day and am dying for something to eat. In my head I'm preparing some salty, greasy dishes while I am walking along on a road that has been freshly cleared by the snow plough.

There's no moon, but the snow lights up the landscape and it's easy to find my way on the last section through the forest. I collect some birch bark on the way. I go into the tent and breathe deeply. It smells of the extinguished fire. It's good to be home.

I make a stew of green lentils and German sausage, and flavour it with thyme and salt. I wolf it all down and crawl into my sleeping bag.

Now I've got everything I need. Now the cold can come.

I want a girl. I want to make out.

ONE EVENING I PUT ON my skis and go out through the darkness up to Norsjön. The ice is thick and I ski out over the lake. Neither moon nor stars in the sky. The fir trees are looming, huge, dark and silent around the edge of the lake.

Even so I am not at peace. Four months of struggle is finally over. In the end I just couldn't fight against it any longer, I had to bow my head and to humbly accept my fear of the dark. Then it disappeared. From one day to the next – no more phantoms behind me.

When I was most afraid, I very nearly moved out of the forest. Now I am happy that I didn't give up.

I stand still enjoying the dark silence out there on the ice, neither restless nor afraid.

Now I see the forest.

EVERYTHING THAT I DO demands an effort. If I want the water to heat up or if something has to dry, I must fix it; no one else will do it for me. Make a fire or go cold, it's as simple as that. I like the clarity.

I make a fire with birch bark and little fir twigs, and I melt snow so I can wash – three litres brought to boiling point. I take off all my clothes and walk naked out of the tent, standing on two logs so that my feet won't get too cold. I put some snow into the hot water until the temperature is just so. I use an old cotton shirt as a flannel, and carefully rub away the dirt from my face and body. There's a cloud of steam around me. I wrap my feet up, go inside and sit down next to the fire and dry out.

I put on dry underwear and thick woollen socks, fill the saucepan with snow and boil the cloth until it's clean. I hang it on a line above the fire to dry.

When I have made my evening porridge, I let the fire burn out. I lie down on my back in bed. My body is relaxing as the sleeping bag helps the blood in my hands and feet to warm up. My face gets cold as soon as the dying fire lowers the temperature inside the tent.

I see my breath being drawn towards the smoke vent. I listen to the muffled sounds of the forest.

There is a restful feeling in the cold and darkness that I have never experienced before. I don't feel any tiredness, I feel a kind of perfect equilibrium. I've never felt so good.

It's as if my thoughts become clearer the colder it gets.

I FOLD BACK THE flap across the opening and go outside. The tent is covered in cold fresh snow. There are no animal tracks, there are no sharp edges, everything is gentle, softened.

I take out my skis that are leaning against a fir tree, put on my rucksack and start skiing towards Järpen. My food has run out, and I must restock. The snow is deep and my progress is slow, but I am happy – it's cold, but I am warm anyway. I still feel my toes and my blood is full of energy.

When I get to the riding school in Järpen three hours later, I am sweating. I put the skis under a tree and I walk the last stretch into the village.

The ICA store is packed out, and it feels strange to see so many people in one place. I haven't spoken to anyone for a month. I'm overwhelmed by the sounds and I absorb it all. I can't resist; my head is full, fit to burst.

I pack the rucksack with enough food for 17 days, pay and go out into the cold. It feels good to be outside again. My sweat-soaked jacket is freezing and my back and hands get cold as I walk back to pick up my skis.

My body begins to warm up as I start to ski homewards, but my hands are still cold. I don't understand why they are not adjusting to the temperature. It's as if they are living their own cold existence beyond my control.

The moon is shining like a warm lightbulb in the sky and I ski alongside my own shadow. I get home a couple of hours later. The forest is deathly silent.

I store my provisions in a wooden box with a lid. There is a hungry mouse living in my woodpile and he likes to pinch my food.

THE FILMMAKER PETER MAGNUSSON pays me a visit. He gets out of the train at Järpen and the snow creaks beneath our feet as we walk along the road to my tent. It's clear and dark outside, the snow and stars are the only sources of light.

He's bringing a camera and a sleeping bag and I lend him another bag and reindeer hide. I prepare a sleeping area for him near the woodpile. We don't talk a lot.

'We'll save that for when we start filming,' he says.

In the night I wake up from Peter kicking me, and there's a panic in his voice as he says that the whole tent is about to collapse. He holds both hands against two of the poles and his voice is stressed as he asks me to help him.

'The whole damn thing is about to come down, Markus.'

'What do you mean?'

'Look at the poles, they're leaning!'

'They're meant to lean,' I laugh. 'The tent is pointed up there and gets wider further down. Go back to sleep, everything is fine.'

I wake up as it gets light the next day. My feet are sore when I put them into the ice-cold boots. I make porridge for us, flavouring it with cinnamon and raisins.

We eat and make a fire and walk about in the forest. Peter films whatever he wants to film, stands still behind the camera and looks all stiff. His camera batteries are playing up, the cold is sapping their power.

I would never have made it as a documentary filmmaker in the winter. I have to keep moving, otherwise I get cold.

I SLEEP UNTIL IT GETS LIGHT, then I feel rested and hungry. My nose is a bit cold, but the rest of my body is comfortably warm. When I lift my head, some hairs have come away from my beard, which has frozen solid and stuck to the pillow.

I light a candle and look at the thermometer: it's -37°C.

My sleeping bag is white and stiff, covered with ice crystals. On the inside the down is starting to lose its shape – my body heat meets the cold outside and produces condensation. At the same time the sleeping bag is too thick for me to be able to dry it over the fire. When I crawl into bed in the evenings, there are little shards of ice inside it, which are uncomfortable to lie on. Down doesn't respond well to moisture.

I don't really know what to do. If the cold persists as it has done for the last couple of weeks, I will soon be really cold at night.

I have two woolly hats on in the night-time and thin woollen underwear. I crawl out of the sleeping bag and put on my clothes really fast. I don't manage to tie both shoelaces before my fingers are so stiff that I have to warm them against my tummy for a moment. I put on my mittens and chip some wood for kindling.

It's difficult to get the fire going; the cold pushes the smoke downwards towards the floor. I go down on all fours and blow on the embers. The smoke gets in my eyes, and my knees are getting cold.

At last the fire takes and the smoke disappears. I sit close up to warm my fingers. I feel the cold draught against my back.

Everything feels good anyway. The cold makes me move fast.

I go out and get some snow. If I fill the whole saucepan, it will be just the right amount of water for a helping of porridge. I pour in the oats and whittle in a piece of frozen butter. I flavour it with cinnamon and dried apricots. I eat until my stomach is full to bursting.

I fill the saucepan with more snow and drink some warm water, then put in a few grains of salt, which makes it taste better. At once I'm desperate for a shit, and I plod quickly into the forest and pull down my trousers, but the snow is a metre thick and it's hard to squat. I manage to dig out a hole with my hands just in time. I dry my bum with a handful of powder snow.

My fingers are unbelievably cold.

THE COLD IN MY BLOOD seems to be constantly supercharging my body. My heart is beating faster.

I have never had to think about the amount of damp and sweat I produce simply by existing. But the colder it gets, the more time I need to spend simply keeping my stuff dry. If my shoes are wet when I go to bed, they will be frozen when I wake up. Every evening my socks are damp. In the beginning I dried them against my stomach overnight. But now I boil water, pour it into a bottle and slide the socks over this before I get into my sleeping bag. That way, they dry faster. I try things out to see what works.

I act on the concrete problems, the ones that I know I have to solve.

I throw snow up onto the tent as added insulation, covering it up like an igloo. If I don't make a fire, it is just as cold inside the tent as outside. I have to work hard to keep warm. I have to be totally in the moment, always listening to the signals that my body is sending. *Can I move my toes? Do my fingers work?* I feel my face for cold patches.

The cold teaches me to listen. It shows me through pain if I'm making a mistake. Clear and direct, but all the same it's difficult: easy for the head, harder for the body. Nothing that has to be done can be postponed. Just to stay alive is like a low-intensity, round-the-clock training session.

I sleep 12 hours a night just to keep going.

I SKI THROUGH THE FOREST trying to keep up a high work rate in my legs, but the snow is so deep that progress is slow. The cold feels like a string tied around my toes.

I'm up here on Romohöjden hill a couple of kilometres from the tent. I'm out of breath, but the warmth isn't happening yet. Good God, it's cold.

I come down to Helgesjön and follow the Slagsån for the final kilometre back home. I go inside, sit on the bed and light a candle.

I take off my boots ands socks and look at my toes. They are white. The soles of my feet look like raw cod flesh.

I'm too cold to take the time to light a fire, I don't think that my toes can cope with the wait. I know what to do, but I've got to act straight away. Either I've got to fix this or I'll lose my toes.

I strip naked, crawl into the sleeping bag and press my toes and the soles of my feet against my warm calves. I pull my head into the sleeping bag and relax. I am thinking only of getting warm. My toes are aching. I put on an extra pair of socks, warming them against my stomach before pulling them over my feet. Slowly but surely, the blood is reaching my toes.

At last I risk getting dressed again. I light a fire and really build it up. I put my chopping block in front of the fire like a stool and warm my feet until they are red.

I'm all warm as I crawl back into the sleeping bag and I cook a meal as I lie there – I try the frozen meat, and grate in some carrots and leeks. I add salt and some snow, and put in an extra knob of butter.

I eat straight from the saucepan, something between a soup and a stew. My whole body is warm, from the stomach outwards.

I PACK MY RUCKSACK with my sleeping bag, sleeping mat, clothes and food and put on my skis. I'm going to Duved to have coffee with Bertil. It's 35 kilometres away.

The snow is unforgiving and progress is slow. There's no wind, but even so I can feel the cold blowing across my arms and back. After 30 minutes I have to stop to get the blood flowing in my arms. My hands are a weak link.

I go past the Björn and slalom down in wide turns towards Åresjön. My skis are wobbly and it's hard to manage a controlled run. My face is frozen by the blasts of icy air. I cover the last 13 kilometres to Duved on the southern side of the Indalsälven.

When I arrive my nose is cold, my lower arms are numb, and my thumbs are frozen. I knock on the door at Bertil and Ingrid's. Ingrid opens. I am so happy that they are in.

They give me hot tea and Ingrid brings out some food. I fill my belly with protein and butter. The warmth makes me feel slow and heavy; my hands are pulsating and my face feels swollen. Bertil tells me that he has just skied 15 kilometres and says that it's important to keep going even when you're a pensioner.

Bertil is still involved with Duved's sports club. He asks how my running is going. He's being very tactful, he knows my history. I tell him that I feel strong and that it is fun to be running again, and I can tell that Bertil is pleased.

He mentions an event in Trondheim in the spring, and says that if I want he'd like to take me there. Bertil and Ingrid have their history as well. It's a few years since their son died, but the grief is still there. It probably always will be.

I say that I'm not sure I'm ready to compete again, we'll see. When I'm warmed through, I fill my thermos with warm water and get ready to leave. I say goodbye and start skiing homewards. Outside it's got dark, but it's not as cold as it was this morning. Life is great.

I pick up my own track back to Åre, working my way up the hill to the Bear. I'm exhausted. I won't have the strength to get all the way home.

I decide to spend the night at the Fröå wind shelter. I take out my sleeping mat and sleeping bag, pull off my boots and my thick outer clothing. I roll up my jacket into a pillow.

I am completely alone and no one knows where I am. If anything happens now, then I'll have to fix it.

I am completely left to my own devices and I like it.

I wake up the next day frozen stiff. I put on my frozen clothes and my stone-hard boots. I drink warm water from the thermos, eat a sandwich that I kept in my sleeping bag, and ski the last 15 kilometres back home.

I'M AWOKEN BY SOMETHING running across my face. The tent is in total darkness.

I light a candle. I see nothing, I hear nothing. It must have been a mouse.

There's ice in my beard and my body's heavy from the cold, but I've finally solved the problem with the sleeping bag. I've bought a thin synthetic bag, which I stretch over the thick downy one. At night the damp travels outwards and ends up in the outer bag and the down stays dry thanks to the warmth from my body. The synthetic bag dries quickly above the fire.

I lie down on my front and go back to sleep.

IN MARCH THE LIGHT RETURNS and the temperature rises. I have got through the coldest part of the year and I've still got all my fingers and toes.

I get up early and ski across the frozen snow of Helgesjön, sliding over the ice. The going is fast and easy, and the sun is warm on my back. I'm wearing a thin sweater and gloves and I'm not cold.

I reach the Helgesjövallen and continue beneath the power line towards Skaltjärn, travelling along frozen scooter tracks. When I get to the lake, I turn off and follow the red crosses marking the mountain path to Norsjön. I can see reindeer tracks. Otherwise I am all alone.

Nature is waking up again and I hear the song of the first birds of spring after the silence of winter. The contrasts are enormous: from silent, cold and dark to light and vibrant life.

I continue across Norsjön and get to the slopes on the other side. I'm sliding on the frozen snow through the forest along a steep downhill path. My legs are wobbly as I race through the trees, excitement bubbling up in my chest – I love reaching a speed where I'm on the verge of losing control.

I get to the foot of the hill and continue through the valley all the way to the tent – and have a feeling of intense happiness, as I always do, when I see it. It's strange that this simple canvas structure can feel so like home. It has protected me from everything: rain, snow and phantoms.

I've had nine months of fulfilling my basic needs and I don't long for anything else. It's been the best winter of my life.

ONE DAY IN APRIL I put on my running shoes and jog down to the big road. I have put away my skis for the season and most of the snow has gone.

I've decided to go with Bertil to the competition in Trondheim, so the time has come for some speed training. I warm up with 15 gentle minutes on the gravelly roads. I do a few sprints, and I plan to run three lots of ten minutes at high speed.

I set off along the road, running past Undersåker church and the parish hall. I push myself, feeling strong but not particularly quick after the winter – I'm not used to moving my legs this fast. I stop and rest for a couple of minutes after the first section. I time myself with a simple Casio watch that I got from Dad.

I run past Hålland, listening to the roar of the Ristafallet. It's the spring flood. I pause after the second section, resting my hands against my knees. As I don't know the exact distances, I can't judge my speed, but it doesn't matter. As long as it's hard work, it will pay dividends.

I push myself to the limit for the last 10 minutes. My legs are really hurting during the uphill run home through the forest. There's still snow under the fir trees, and I jog slowly at the end. It feels good to finish on a soft surface.

I hang up my running shoes over a clothes line when I get home and ring out my socks and hang them beside the shoes. I go down to the Slagsån and jump in while I still feel the warmth in my body. The freshly melted water is so cold that my whole body starts to ache. I soap myself from top to toe and rinse myself quickly before running up to the tent and wrapping myself in a blanket.

I get out a carton of yoghurt, treating myself to a bit of bacterial culture now that it isn't so cold any more. When I try to pour the yoghurt into my bowl nothing comes out. That's odd because I can feel from the weight of the carton that there's a lot left there. I squeeze a bit harder but the contents just don't want to come out. There must be some kind of plug. I give it a proper squeeze and the plug is loosened and the yoghurt comes out.

I sprinkle on some nuts and stir. Then at last I can see the plug: a hairy little mouse. Drowned in my supper.

THE WET GRAVEL STICKS to the soles of my boots as I walk along the road down to the E14. Here spring has really arrived. I hold up my thumb and I quickly get a lift all the way to Duved. Bertil is waiting for me and we get into his old grey Mercedes and drive across the mountain, past Storlien and over the Norwegian border, towards the Trondheim fjord.

Nature gets greener the closer we get to the fjord. I can feel the smell of salt and there are sea birds in the sky. I am missing the west coast and Öckerö, and yet I don't want to go there.

The race starts in a schoolyard that is high up on a hill. Bertil is wearing his overalls in the colours of Duved's sports club and he's in an upbeat mood. We are the only Swedes among a lot of Norwegians. It's two years since I last competed and it feels weird to be surrounded by so many people again.

I warm up and do my sprints. My body responds. I feel calm inside. It's actually going to be quite fun to run fast.

The starting pistol fires and I'm off – the race is a little less than 12 kilometres along the streets of Trondheim. It feels comfortable and I pull away from the leaders. I'm soon running on my own. After four kilometres I see Bertil on the sidelines cheering me on. I check out my own reflection in the shop windows and there is no one coming up behind me.

AFTER NINE KILOMETRES, THERE IS a long uphill section – my legs are hurting and my arms are starting to feel heavy. At the top of the hill some officials shout that there's only 1.5 kilometres to go. I relax and push myself as hard as I can for this last section. I reach the finishing line in 37 minutes and I feel no pain at all.

I win two kilos of brunost [Norwegian brown cheese]. Wonderful! It's a long time since I had any cheese.

Bertil and I go back across the mountain into Åredalen. He drops me off in Hålland and I walk slowly through the forest back to the tent. The adrenaline is starting to recede and my body feels heavy.

Back at home I hang up my sweaty running clothes, light a fire and make some tea. I treat myself to some crispbread with thick, thick slices of brown cheese.

THE SKY IS GREY, rain is on its way and the west wind is blowing hard. It's 12°C outside. In my rucksack I've got shorts, running spikes and a running vest; crispbread, water and nuts. I'm standing with my thumb raised beside the E14, trying to hitch a lift to Krokom to do some interval training on the running track. Nobody stops.

Perhaps my beard is too unkempt. I probably look like a murderer.

After 45 minutes I get a lift, but only to Mörsil. Still 30 miles to go. Again I am standing with my thumb in the air and nobody wants to pick me up. At long last a building worker who's finished for the day stops, and he's going all the way to Östersund.

I jump off at Krokom and walk the final kilometre to the running track. When I get there, it's quite deserted. I change and warm up by jogging four kilometres on the floodlit track next door.

I put on my spikes and do some sprints on the Tartan track. It feels really strange. I haven't done any interval training on a track since the camp in Austria.

I'm planning on running 15 lots of 400 metres with a minute's rest between each one. The aim is to run each interval in less than 70 seconds.

I run off and it feels heavy at once. I have no speed in my body. After five intervals it's really hard going, but then it turns round. I start to recognise my body, and I run with light legs and stiff calves. I find the speed. I'm pleased when I've finished. This was fun.

I jog for four kilometres, change and walk over to the E14 to hitch-hike back again. I eat my crispbread and nuts, and I feel a great sense of calm inside me. Nobody stops. The rain arrives and I put on my raincoat. It does feel a bit tough. I want to get back home now. Seventy kilometres is too far to walk.

At last a Norwegian stops on his way to Trondheim. He plays Mogwai on his CD player and I listen avidly. It's been a long time since I heard any music.

When I have jumped out in Hålland and am walking across the hill in my white raincoat with the hood pulled up, the music continues to echo inside my head. What a day!

THE BIRDS ARE SINGING AWAY, the evening sun shines through the fir trees and I'm sitting outside preparing some food. The smoke from the fire rises straight up. Not a breath of wind. I'm frying onions and potatoes in butter using a long stick as a makeshift spatula. My heart rate is normal, one-and-a-half seconds between each beat.

I take the saucepan off the fire, pour in a tin of tuna and season with some black pepper and salt. I eat and then lie down to rest on the reindeer skin.

I'm thinking about God. Why is he so silent? Am I being deceived or does he actually exist?

The forest falls silent. Someone must be approaching.

A moment later Jocke comes walking along the edge of the forest. He's a lad I got to know when I was studying in Hålland. I dig out a spare reindeer hide and prepare some mint tea. I don't get many visitors, so it's always great when someone drops in.

We sit chatting by the fire. We talk about making an effort, and about learning to be satisfied with very little, about doing without in order to appreciate life even more. The simple life as a door leading into one's heart.

When it starts getting dark, Jocke goes back home. I light some tea lights and go down to the river. I can just see the soft light from the tent between the fir trees as I wash myself.

I shake off most of the water on the way back and shiver as I creep into my sleeping bag. I blow out the candles as I wait for sleep to come.

Bloody hell, life is good.

THE BIRCHES HAVEN'T YET got their new leaves, but it's about to happen. I run through the forest, ducking below the branches. It's raining and I'm wet, but I'm not cold. The rain is mild.

At the college in Hålland I ask to borrow the telephone. I haven't spoken to Grandad for a while. Grandma answers.

'Grandad is asleep,' she says. 'He's been out fishing mackerel all night. The whole basement stinks of fish.'

'As per usual,' I say.

We chat about Mum for a bit, about how she's mostly resting on the sofa, about how weird it feels that she's so sick. Then Grandma says, 'Markus, what are you actually playing at? Why are you living alone in the forest? I mean, we're not in the Stone Age any more. When I was a child I had to get water from the well and carry in the wood every day. It was really hard work. It's great not to have to do those things any more.'

► Me and my siblings (Elin on Mum's lap, Ida with the blonde hair, Gustav on my lap) on the sofa, six months before Mum fell ill. Mum didn't like having her picture taken, which is why she's looking away from the camera.

© Private collection

◄ Just finished my first race, a 10 kilometre circuit around Öckerö island, where I grew up. I'm 10 and I love the feeling of my legs being tired and sore.

© Private collection

► I'm chopping wood with the hatchet Grandad gave me. Always on the east side of the tent to avoid those western winds.

© Soren Marklund

▶ Winter is coming. I'm filling up the tent with firewood, which should last for a couple of weeks.

© Soren Marklund

▶ The first snow of the season and I can still get around without skis. Always great to lift the tent flap and smell the smoke.

© Peter Magnusson/helionfilm

▼ Running up the two kilometre track to the top of Mount Romohöjden.

© Peter Magnusson/helionfilm

© Peter Magnusson/helionfilm

▲ Long training session (27 kilometres from Väliste mountain to the tent). The first 10 kilometres are a comfortable downhill run.

▸ Deep snow-walking, 25 degrees below. Exhausting. Two minutes' walk, one minute's rest. I do this 15 times.

© Peter Magnusson/helionfilm

▸ Spring is here, and the winter and snow are on their way out. I can run across the marshes but they are still very cold. The ice has gone, but the cold stings my body when I wash myself.

© Peter Magnusson/helionfilm

© Peter Magnusson/helionfilm

▲ Sprinting on the road between Gunnivallen and Helgesjövallen. It's summer, but the air is cool, so I am wearing a woolly hat.

© Peter Magnusson/helionfilm

◄ Moving the tent, dragging the poles to the new clearing. Twenty-two poles, four at a time, my arms getting grazed.

▼ Summer running in the nearby woods, along animal tracks, up hills and across brooks.

© Peter Magnusson/helionfilm

▼ First meeting with the runners in Tanzania. I'm just meeting Naftal (in the pink shirt), the best of the group. He's a bit shy, doesn't say much, but he's always cheerful. I'll be sharing a room with Naftal.

© Peter Magnusson/helionfilm

© Peter Magnusson/helionfilm

▼ Long training session across coffee plantations. Everyone warmly dressed to lose weight in the heat. I am wearing a woolly hat, tights and jacket.

▲ First speed training in Tanzania. Blood not yet adjusted to the altitude. Struggle to keep up. Shaving my head no help.

© Peter Magnusson/helionfilm

▲ On Välaberget,
late summer. The air
is cool; it looks like
rain. I used to go
there often for the
view. Väliste hill is
in the background.

▼ The trumpet
was with me for
those four years in
the forest. It was
good to play some
favourite tunes
now and again.

© Peter Magnusson/helionfilm

© Peter Magnusson/helionfilm

▲ Washing myself in the Slagsån.
Not such an effort in summer, harder
in winter when the cold shrinks your
prick and numbs your feet.

◄ Reading with new-born Birgitta on my front. The smell of a new baby and a good book – an unbeatable combination.

▼ Summer on Öckerö. Helga is in the background.

▼ Late summer 2014 by Lake Helgesjön. Jämtland's warmest summer in living memory. The water in the lake was 23 degrees. Åreskutan in the background. Frida and the children having a lovely time.

Vertical text in right margin: © Private collection

© Matti Rapila Andersson

© Private collection

◄ Distance running around the mountain pastures, along the scooter track in non-rustling clothes, woolly hat and cotton jacket.

▲ Noses and ears never stop growing. Looking at this picture, I think my nose will be enormous in 40 years or so. Think Gerard Depardieu.

▼ Distance running across the Öckerö rocks. I love running on untouched terrain, where I have to clamber and jump to get through.

'I understand,' I say. 'But the forest and the darkness and the cold are helping me to find my direction.'

'What sort of nonsense is that? Can't you do that when you live normally?'

'I don't think so.'

'I just don't understand you, Markus. Why must you always exaggerate like that? Why can't you be like other people?'

'I don't know,' I say. 'I've got to go now. Love to Grandad.'

The sky is dark when I run back through the forest. I understand that Grandma thinks I'm weird, and that my life seems to be going backwards. But I am living here because I want to. I don't live off anyone else. I manage with very limited means. And my head is calm, not crammed with all kinds of thoughts.

AN OLD MAN GIVES ME A LIFT all the way from Undersåker to Edsåsdalen. We are driving with the windows down, the sun is beating down from a blue sky. I am wearing running shoes and shorts and I'm bare-chested, with a thin woollen jersey tied round my waist. I jump out just outside Köjagården and start to run.

I get right down to the bottom of the valley where the ski tracks normally start. I run the path all the way to the Offsjöarna, and after three kilometres on the dirt track I turn off and take the forest path up towards the summit. The ground is marshy, wet and heavy going. When it gets too exhausting to run, I start walking. It's tough but it feels good, and gentle on the legs. Nothing hurts.

I manage the whole trek up to the summit, sit down on the stone marker and pull on my jersey. There are mountains in every direction. The Ottfjället, dark, steep and close. The Bunnerfjällen far away in the distance.

I see the whole world. I see everything that is worth looking after, worth preserving.

I start to run across the marsh that angles downwards from the summit. I run fast on the downhill slope, increasing my speed until I lose control, fall over and slide on my stomach over the muddy grass and am soaked to the skin. I get up, carry on running and laugh aloud to myself.

I'm feeling a bit crazy. Am I losing it?

I don't give a damn.

I lose control again and slip down into a muddy hollow. This is life. I'm completely consumed by nature.

I get down from the mountain, turn off the path and run all the way to Edsåsdalen. When I'm back where I started, after 15 kilometres of hard running, I lie down by the stream. I let the cold water wash over me until I'm clean and I stay there until my body starts to feel stiff.

I stroll homewards through the village, using the warm air as my towel. The sun is shining straight into my eyes.

When I pass Köjagården, I start jogging. I've got 15 kilometres to go. I run five kilometres until I get to Edsåshöjden. My stomach feels completely empty and I need to fill up with some water sweetened with honey and some oatmeal. I hear the sound of a car, put up my thumb and get a lift all the way to the E14. Great, only four kilometres left. I run with heavy legs over Romohöjden, across the marsh and up to the Slagsån. When I get home, my shoes and shorts are still wet.

My brain is whirring nicely, I'm tired, happy and seriously hungry.

I wash in the river, and make a fire in the tent, which chases away the mosquitoes. I close the flap and make myself the world's most delicious oatmeal porridge, relishing every mouthful. I drink a whole litre of honey-water with a bit of salt added.

I lie down on the bed. I don't think about anything at all.

I don't feel any longing for anything at all.

I am completely content.

I RUN HOME TO JOCKE in Hålland and borrow the telephone. It's an eternity before mum answers. I can see her in front of me, lying on the sofa with a carer holding the receiver for her.

She sounds tired, but still pleased to hear my voice. I ask her if she's been using her roller skates.

'Not yet, God is as stubborn as ever. I don't understand why he's so quiet. Do you think he's going to make me well?'

'I hope so,' I say.

'Surely it can't be so difficult to make my legs work again?'

'Perhaps we can give Ulf a ring and hear what he's got to say? Maybe he's got some suggestion.'

'I think we'll give that a miss,' says Mum.

'OK.'

AT THE END OF JUNE I take part in the St Olav run for the Duved sports club. It's a relay race between Östersund and Trondheim, where you're in a team of ten who run up to six miles each every day for four days. We are demolished by an African team. Although they look as if they're taking it really easy, their time is an hour better than ours when we reach the finishing line in Trondheim.

When I see them run, I ask myself what I'm doing. They run with such incredible ease, as if they don't need to make any sort of effort. Beside them I feel like an elephant.

I fall in love with the way they move. If I could only learn to run like that.

After the race, Bertil and I go up to their coach. I ask him if I can go back home with them and train alongside them. He answers, 'When do you want to come and how long do you want to stay?'

'October,' I say. 'I want to stay over the winter, perhaps six months.'

'That's fine. Get a plane to Nairobi, then take a coach to Arusha, which is in Tanzania. We train in a village near there. Just send us an email so we know when you're arriving. I'll get one of the runners to pick you up at the coach station.'

So that's that.

BACK HOME IN THE TENT I pull the synthetic sleeping bag over me like a blanket. It's night-time but still light. The air is damp, and I'm thinking of the sea.

It feels a bit unreal that I'm going to fly down there and train with some of the best runners in the world. Perhaps my decision was a little hasty, but it feels right.

I've got to get the money together for the trip. I should be able to get by on about 12,000 kronor [$1,385]: 1000 kronor [$115] a month for food and lodging, 600 kronor [$70] for the return flight. I fall asleep with the blanket over my face and don't wake up until the sun is high in the sky the next day.

I run down into the village and call my cousin who works in a factory making garage doors, and ask him if he can fix me up with a job. No problem, he says. They always need people who are up for work.

I FOLD UP THE CANVAS THAT MAKES UP the tent and put it away in a red plastic box, and I carry the poles into the forest and lean them up against a big fir tree. I stuff my sleeping bag into my rucksack, roll up my three reindeer skins and tie them on the outside with some strong cord. I place the camping stove on top of the sleeping bag.

This is the equipment that I am concerned about, the stuff that I've been able to buy because I've been economising and going hungry. It's worth 800 kilos of porridge oats and I want to keep it safely indoors while I'm in Tanzania, or else the mice and the voles will get at it.

All the rest – spices, olive oil, thick woollen trousers, my winter boots, the axe and the saw – I stuff into a black bin liner, which

I secure tightly to the trunk of a fir tree so that the dense and heavy branches can protect it from the rain and snow. I put the bed under another fir tree and use the horsehair mattress as a protective cover.

I put on my rucksack, put the plastic box on my shoulder, wade across the Slagsån and make my way through the forest to Hålland. I sneak into the college and put my things at the back of the storage behind the skiing equipment without asking for permission.

I will spend a month installing garage doors on Hisingen in Gothenburg. Then: Africa.

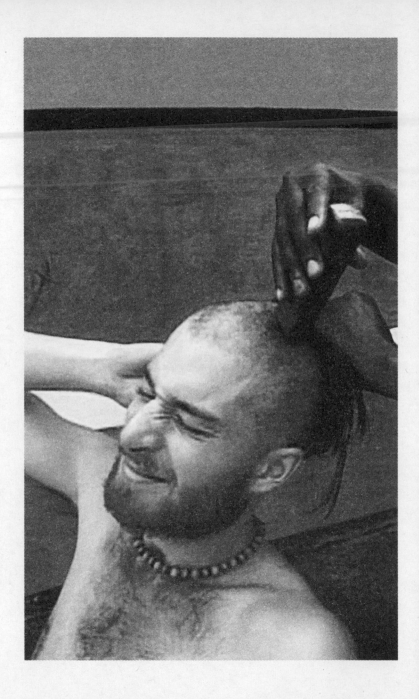

TANZANIA

AFTER EIGHT HOURS in the air, I am desperate to stretch my legs. Peter, the documentary filmmaker, is fast asleep in the seat next to me. He's going to film my first days in Tanzania.

I bought my tickets through the students travel agency Kilroy Travels – 5500 kronor [$635] return Göteborg Landvetter–Nairobi. I've got 6000 kronor [$690] in travellers' cheques and 500 kronor [$60] in cash.

I feel nervous as we leave the plane. The air is thin and warm and smells different. I collect my 50-litre rucksack from the baggage carousel and it still smells of smoke from my tent. A thousand memories wash over me: darkness, cold, me warm in the sleeping bag, alone with my calm heartbeat.

The rucksack contains everything I will need for the upcoming six months: two pairs of running shoes, running shorts, long tights, a thick cotton sweater, two pairs of long johns, three pairs of socks and woollen underwear; two books by Dostoevsky, *The Idiot* and *Crime and Punishment*; a cheap CD player and some Mogwai and Low CDs; a new diary with unlined pages. Apart from that, only the clothes I'm wearing and the anorak that I've tied around my waist. Peter and I work our way through the crowd outside passport control, looking for the bus that will take us over the border to Tanzania. We find ourselves in another world. I'm not used to airports, they stress me out. I can feel my Adam's apple straining as I breathe before we find our bus.

We buy our tickets, set off and bump along through Nairobi's teeming streets and out into the countryside. I calm down as soon as I can see a bit further. I'll never get used to the urban environment. I can see grass and open fields with giraffes and water buffalo. A dark green horizon far away.

We reach Arusha at early light. There's a sea of humanity as we get off the bus. No asphalt, just compacted earth. Gentle on the feet. Peter and I are the only light-skinned ones around, and people come right up to us to have a look. That's OK.

My rucksack is covered in a film of red dust when the bus driver chucks it down from the roof. I take a deep breath and suppress my anxiety. Peter is standing to the side filming, a silent eye that watches and preserves images.

I feel the hunger in my stomach. I haven't eaten for ages, I've only drunk tepid water. I catch sight of a gangling young guy who is holding up a sign with my name on. I hold out my hand to him.

'Hello, my name is Markus.'

'Hello, Markos, my name is Thadey.'

'Not Markos, Markus.'

'Markos?'

OK, I think to myself, I'm going to be Markos here.

'The coach asked me to pick you up,' says Thadey.

After that we don't say much more. Thadey's English vocabulary seems very limited. We walk out of the town and follow a red dirt path up the slopes towards Mount Meru, 4565 metres high.

'You're going to be training and living on this mountain,' says Thadey.

We pass simple houses with tin roofs and small tables where people are selling mango, papaya, pineapple and bananas. There are banana trees with huge green leaves in every garden, children shouting '*Mzungu! Mzungu!*'

'It means "white man",' explains Thadey.

Everyone greets us with a wide smile. The children are barefoot and wear shorts and long-sleeved shirts. Everyone has close-cropped hair.

It's great to shake off the stiffness in my legs. The air is thinner than I'm used to. Arusha is at 1800 metres and we are ascending with every step. I've not adjusted yet. I can feel something different in my body. My heart rate is going at a few extra beats per minute.

After three kilometres we're there: two low cemented houses with an open space between, and a black water pump in the middle of the yard. No view, there are trees in the way. Between the trees I can see some wooden seats and an outside toilet with three doors painted blue.

All around there are little brick houses, each with its own patch of grass. It's like Öckerö, but the houses are smaller and the gardens are bigger. There's more foliage, which stops people from looking in.

The coach Zakharias introduces me to his wife Mama Gwandu and tells me that she has run in two Olympic Games. Then I meet the other runners: Naftal, Dominic, Patrick, Dam Dam, Jackson, Farida and Zakia. Zakharias and Mama Gwandu have also got four children, who all watch me with intense curiosity.

Zakharias is the only one with good English. Naftal knows a few words and the others just keep nodding and looking pleased. I recognise some of them from the relay race to Trondheim. They are all small and thin, and beside them I feel huge and white.

The room I am given has blank green walls and no electricity. Just two bunks with green mosquito nets and a few hooks on the wall. I will be sharing the room with Naftal.

'Perfect,' I say. 'I'll sleep well here.'

I'm left alone and unpack my clothes. I've got two hooks, and that's enough. I put my running shoes inside the door and lie down on the bed. On the outside I can hear a pig snuffling against the wall.

A moment later I'm woken up by Zakharias, who says that we'll soon be eating.

'And, Markos, you have to boil the water before you drink it. Otherwise: big problems. You will get typhoid and amoeba.'

In the kitchen the children and all the runners are sitting on wooden seats around a low table. A naked lightbulb is dangling from the ceiling. Mama Gwandu is preparing food over coal. It smells of fire. Just like home.

She serves me up a big portion of corn porridge with beans – like oatmeal porridge but thicker. Suits me perfectly. The meal is rounded off with big cups of black tea with lots of sugar. I feel right at home.

I say thanks for the meal and go to bed. Night has fallen. It's dark like Jämtland in the autumn. I hear the pig outside the window. I keep the mosquitoes out with a net. I don't take the malaria medicine. I've heard that it can affect you mentally. That's not for me. I want to be clean.

THE COACH WAKES ME UP with a knock at the door.

'Markos, time to get up!'

I put on my shorts and vest and tie up my running shoes. Outside it's cool and damp and heavy drops are falling from the trees. Everything feels freshly showered. Light arrives quickly – just a few breaths, and the sky changes from the dark of the night to the morning sun.

The other runners are already there. Zakharias tells us how we're going to train.

'You are doing distance today: *pole pole*. Run the Sanawari circuit. Don't forget that it's *pole pole*.'

Pole pole? I am told that this means calm in Swahili. Great, my legs are still heavy after the flight. We're off. I've no idea how long the Sanawari circuit is, but the speed is low and I am tripping along easily.

After a couple of kilometres, I am starting to feel the pressure. Maybe the speed has increased a bit? My legs are still heavy. After a few more kilometres the speed is obviously faster. What are they playing at? It's meant to be *pole pole*! We run on, it's faster and faster, successive accelerations kilometre after kilometre. I begin to feel worn out, but I've got to keep up because I have no idea where I am.

Everything looks the same: red paths and lush greenery.

My legs are hurting and I'm falling behind. I am gritting my teeth, but I simply can't keep up. I'm making my maximum effort, but that's not enough. My lungs are working away in my ribcage, but I am losing metre after metre.

The others are running in a big group and are pressing hard on the upward slopes and flow downhill easily at high speed. Each and every one of them runs faster than the fastest Swede. And there I am myself, big and white and 30 metres behind them. People shout '*Mzungu, mzungu!*' when I pass.

One of the runners up ahead points at an empty area right behind his legs. He waves me on and points distinctly at that spot. Presumably he wants me to be there instead of running on my own, but I am going at my maximum speed and the runners up ahead don't decrease theirs.

We are running kilometre after kilometre, and eventually I lose sight of them. I feel completely at a loss. I've focused only on trying to keep up. Great, I get lost on my first day and will soon be eaten by a lion.

I don't see a living person any longer and I don't see any houses. I don't hear any noise apart from birdsong. It's beautiful. But it's also stressful.

I carry on in the same direction for a bit longer. At last I see a runner who's waiting for me beside the path. It's Naftal, the one who knows a bit of English.

'Markos, tired? Today you tired, tomorrow me tired. It's OK.'

We carry on at a gentler pace.

'It's Jackson who always raises the speed. No matter what the trainer says we run calm. Always a little crazy when he's with us.'

We run homewards, side by side. The trainer is waiting for us after the session. He's drinking tea and looking pleased. We're doing some strength training with homemade weights while Peter stands to the side filming us.

'Markos, everything is in your head,' says Zakharias. 'You must think. If you are tired, so are the others. Just hang in there, and refuse to give up. That is what you're training must be about, to keep up.'

I fill up a bucket with cold water and rinse myself. I wash my running kit and hang it up to dry on a line between two trees. I drink some tepid water and can feel the emptiness in my stomach.

An hour or so later, Mama Gwandu brings me a cup of corn gruel. I pour in lots of sugar and drink it up. I'm still hungry.

It's great to have Peter there at the beginning, someone to talk with when everything is new. But after a few days he leaves to do some filming in Zanzibar.

Now I am the only *mzungu* left.

WE ARE WORKING HARD ON an upward climb that feels terribly long. We've been running uphill non-stop for 80 minutes and we still haven't reached the top of the hill.

It's over 30°C outside and I am wearing a lot of clothes: long tights, woolly sweater, anorak and a knitted hat. Everything in order to lose fluids and shed some weight. Everyone in the group is doing the same – for the long sessions, we always have to wear a lot of clothes.

I have never worked this way before – rather the opposite, in fact. I like to feel the outdoor temperature directly against my skin. But now I follow their example.

After 90 minutes we get to the woods just below the Merus treeline. Naftal tells me to put on my hat.

'There are snakes in the trees around here that will jump down and bite your head if it's not covered. They're venomous and you'll die straight away.'

I pull on my knitted cotton hat and carry on through the trees. My body is starting to boil; I can feel it in my temples. We are running without water, never drinking while we train. The coach says that we must learn to run without filling up with any fluids or food.

Between the trees we can see the snow up on the top of the mountain. A strange contrast: tropical heat and white cold. I just want to run over there and stuff a snowball under my sweater to feel the cold against my skin.

We continue through the forest. No snakes from the trees. Easy pace. The whole group is bunched up and quiet. Some are more exhausted than others, I can see it in their red eyes. I am longing for cold apple juice mixed with some sparkling water. We keep on running.

After 2 hours 40 minutes, we get back home. I feel several kilos lighter as I pump up a bucket of cold water and have a rinse in the shower room. I pour scoop after scoop over my head. I'm shivering. I fetch some more water and boil away the amoebas and the typhoid. It feels really weird to drink warm water after a long training session under a burning sun.

I WAKE UP WITH THE LIGHT. A moment later, the coach knocks on the door. Another day another session. I open the metal shutter and go outside. I don't like to lock myself in, but Zakharias says that the rumours about a 'rich' *mzungu* are spreading fast, so I might as well be careful.

Zakharias looks tired. He gulps down his beer in the evenings, and pays the price in the mornings. He gives his balls a good old scratch, and straightens his back until it crunches and tells us how we're going to be training.

'Today you're going to do some hill running, the short one over there by the field. Warm up for half an hour and we'll meet up there.'

We jog off, well wrapped up, for a slow uphill run. We pass some barking dogs running loose. They are totally lethal. If you look them in the eye, they attack you.

We get to the hill and jump up and down for a bit. Zakharias is already there. The hill is 100 metres long and very steep. I peel off my top layer and start off without knowing how many ascents we are going to make. If you ask Zakharias, he just says, 'Don't you worry about that, just keep up.'

Not to tell is part of his training philosophy.

I run with short strides and raised knees. I press hard up the hill and use the jog back downhill as a rest. No one in the group has a watch. Up and down, time after time.

'Looks good, Markos,' says Zakharias. 'Just keep up.'

10 runs. 20, 30, 40 . . . 50.

'Well done,' says Zakharias. 'You've finished now.'

We jog back at a gentle pace past the neighbouring village. My legs are light and I feel strong and hungry.

I've been here for two months and my ribs are starting to show. I'm thinking of food the whole time and longing for a cheesecake and oily fish from Bohuslän. But I hold back, even when I've got food in front of me. I have to be lighter in order to run as fast as the others. I can't see any other way.

When we get back home, I drink a litre of tepid water, which I boiled the evening before. I've started to do that and I keep the water in a steel bucket with a lid so that the cockroaches can't get at it. I eat a banana and drink a glass of corn gruel. I want to have more, but I suppress the urge.

I keep my mouth closed as I wash myself with the typhoidal and amoebic water. I sit down on the stone steps outside my room and let the sun dry me. I wash my socks with some newly acquired yellow lemon soap. I try in vain to rub away the red soil from the socks.

I go inside and lie down on my bed, pop in my earpieces and listen to music. I can't stop thinking about which sort of jam I would like with the cheesecake.

NAFTAL IS ACROSS THE ROOM SNOOZING away, his mouth open, while Dominic, Dam-Dam and Patrick are asleep in the room on the other side of the wall. The three share one enormous bed. Farid shares a room with Mama Gwandu and Zakharias. I can't see how they manage to make any more children.

Zakia and Jackson found a way, though, and when Zakia got pregnant they had to leave the group. Zakia is one of the best female runners in the area and has won several European races. She'll probably never run again.

I don't talk so much with anyone, but I still feel involved. Everyone is easy-going, cheerful and kind.

Naftal is the fastest runner. His skin is very shiny and his eyes are light brown. He has stone-hard muscles and an incredible sprint and hasn't dropped out of a single session. He usually wears a knitted hat when he runs. One of his ears sticks out a little. Dominic has a slight crouch when he runs, his arms hanging low. He has a very unusual mouth. His lips are extremely dark and when he smiles he shows his bottom teeth. He likes a high, even speed right from the start, and that's when he produces his best. He has become more tired during my stay here, and he often falls back a few metres behind Naftal. Dominic often helps with the cooking and seems to like that.

Dam-Dam is always cheerful. He has kind eyes and white teeth that are always on show. He runs in rustling tracksuit bottoms, and performs well in the short interval training. Patrick is Zakharias's cousin and a very gentle person. He's always keen to melt into the background. He's a terrific talent but is often sick. Farida is tiny and slight and always very aggressive in his running. She pushes herself until she hits the wall and has to let go. She gives everything she has in every session.

I give Zakharias $100 a month for board and lodging, which is what I lived on in Sweden. The money I'm left with makes it possible for me to go down to Arusha and indulge in the luxury of a glass of orange juice. There I also buy one tube of toothpaste a week, which I share with the others. Before I came, they cleaned their teeth with fresh twigs.

The running system in Tanzania is built on contributions from earlier running champions. They were so gifted that they got to races in other parts of the world, where they won prize money that they brought home and used to build their own house. Often they also build a second house where talented runners can come to live and train for free. Youngsters are given a couple of years in which they can focus exclusively on running.

Those who really progress get themselves overseas off their own bat, and there earn their own money. In turn they pay their dues by building up new careers after their own careers have ended. Those who don't progress will have to find themselves a different career.

Sometimes sponsors will help. It may be earlier members of the group who share their prize money, or people who simply want to do a good deed. Zakharias's team has a Swedish sponsor from Gagnef, who now and then contributes $50–100 per athlete a month. I don't know who he is, I'm told only that he does it with his heart.

A bit away from us lives Team Maxi, with whom we sometimes train. They have two runners who do the half-marathon in under an hour and who are just a bit faster than Naftal. It is unreal to see them run. Easy, easy, without any visible effort, all the time relaxed, their faces totally calm. Their pace never falters due to lactic acid; they always stay on the right side of their own limits.

During the training season the different teams live and train in the hills of Tanzania and Kenya, where they build up their strength and fitness on the soft red paths. Their blood is strengthened by the thin air. They run and rest, day after day. They do nothing else. They don't watch TV and they don't read books.

Then the best of them disappear to the States, Asia or Europe, where they'll find the best prize money.

THE WHITE MINIBUS leaves a black cloud behind it. 'When the exhaust looks like that, then the engine is kaput,' Dad would have said. There are 20 of us in the taxi. Naftal is sitting on my lap, and Dominic on his. I feel Naftal's bony behind digging into my thighs.

We are on our way to the coffee plantation a short distance away towards the Kenyan border. There is a qualification race for the world cross-country championship, and Naftal and Dominic are going to run. The best runners in the country are taking part, and I am there just to look and learn.

The distance is six times round a two-kilometre circuit. We've been there for interval training, so I know what the track is like: a wide path with no slopes, and with trees on either side to protect against the sun.

They're off, and go flat out from the start. After the first circuit Naftal and Dominic are well placed, not at the front but just behind the leaders. I'm standing next to all the coaches. Everyone is relaxed, there are no stressed faces or loud screams. The laps go by.

The race is fast, the swift, light legs floating across the ground. When there are two laps to go, Dominic is beginning to look tired, but Naftal is still hanging in there. With 200 metres remaining of the fifth circuit, someone shouts out to Naftal that he has to start putting a spurt on. I see Naftal between the trees. He ups the speed at once and starts to run at full pelt. His legs are pumping, his shoulders are relaxed. He gains on the leader, and when there are 50 metres to go, he increases his speed even further. He's now going at his absolute max. With 20 metres to go to the finishing line, he's just five metres behind and the distance is shrinking. I wonder what he's up to – after all, he still has one circuit left, but now every coach is screaming: 'Faster, Naftal, FASTER!'

Naftal is in the zone, he thinks that he's almost there. I recognise his expression – the happiness when you think that everything has gone really well. Naftal crosses the finishing line in second place and raises his hands. His face is so happy and relaxed. Then all the trainers start laughing and someone screams that there is still one lap to go. Zakharias is laughing so hard he can barely stand up. I laugh as well. It seems so incredibly funny when Naftal, looking amazed, stumbles off again on stiff legs.

Naftal laughs when he finally crosses the finishing line, this time in eighth place. He realises that he's been tricked. All the trainers come up to slap him on the back and the atmosphere is warm. It was Naftal who made the whole competition, although he didn't manage to get to the cross-country championship.

Running is how Naftal makes his living, but there is also a strong sense that there's something else that is just as important. Perhaps that's the secret, the thing that makes them so good.

I'M SITTING ON MY OWN on the wooden seat under the eaves. I'm wearing a thick sweater and long trousers, but I'm still cold. I've got a temperature. I'm drinking warm water so that the taste of sick and the burning in my throat will go away – I've vomited four times in the last hour. There's only bile left.

I feel really awful. I hate stomach aches more than anything.

The rainy season has started and I see the lightning above Kilimanjaro in the distance to the east. I can't understand how there can be so much lightning – there must be a lot of rage up there in heaven. I wonder what it would be like to do a parachute jump through those clouds, to fly in the rain with arms outstretched between the flashes.

I wish this bloody pain in my stomach would pass. I don't want to be here right now. I am longing to be lying in the sun on a warm rock. I am longing for Mum.

WE HEAD OFF ON THE DAY'S first distance run, jogging along the path near the house. After 50 metres, I spot someone lying face down on the ground. When we get closer I see that he has a big hole in the back of his head. Someone must have beaten him to death. It's the first time I've seen a dead person close up. The skin looks different. It's damp from the dew. I don't know what to do, but no one seems to care and we run on. After a while Naftal says, 'Markos, he's dead. We can't do anything.'

We follow the narrow path up the hill. I focus on keeping my shoulders down. We press on hard on the slopes, but I keep up. I feel hungry but also strong. I don't know where the energy comes from.

When we come back two hours later, the man is still on the path. Someone has turned him over. There he lies with his eyes closed, wearing a dirty T-shirt. We run home.

A little later four men pass by with the dead man. They are carrying him by his arms and legs, and his head bounces up and down as they walk towards the village. Nobody knew who he was. Nobody recognised him.

I do some stretches, eat a banana, and drink a cup of gruel with a lot of sugar in. I'm filling up the rest of my stomach with water. My stomach feels full, but my body is still hungry.

I lie down on the bed and everything feels unreal. Someone has been beaten to death 50 metres from my bedroom window and I didn't hear a thing. I wonder if his family will ever find out why he disappeared.

I SLEEP BADLY. Although I'm tired when I lie down, something keeps whirring inside my head and keeps waking me up, some kind of irritant that is making me overheat. I sleep and wake up, sleep and wake up. I get out of bed in the night to pump up cold water to rinse away the warmth.

I am starting to hear the mosquitoes more clearly. My body feels electrified. It's as if I'm about to be eaten up from within.

When I try to explain it to Zakharias, he says that this is just a good sign, that I must get up and have a cold shower.

'*Shape will come*, Markos.'

I doubt that he's right, but I carry on.

I AM SITTING WITH ZAKHARIAS among the trainers alongside the running track at Arusha stadium. Interval training on the track. All the area's best runners are there: Naftal and Dominic from my group and another twenty or so from elsewhere. Next to me is the former 10,000-metre world record holder on asphalt tracks. He looks uncannily like Morgan Freeman, even the same freckled face – they could be brothers.

He often comes up to us in the evenings for a beer. The alcohol makes him and Zakharias talk in loud voices. I don't understand a lot of what they say, but I get the general drift about old races that they ran abroad many years ago when they were in the best shape of their lives. I add stuff in my imagination, thinking that they are talking about how their running was so easy and relaxed and how they crushed their opponents in the last kilometres of every race. Or started out really fast and just ground down their opposition. Stories from another time that is still so close to their hearts. I love to see all these memories shine in their eyes.

The runners ahead of us are doing 600-metre intervals. The speed is incredibly high. It's like a compact black cloud that whooshes around the track lap after lap. After each interval they jog for 200 metres of rest, silent and focused. Then they're off again.

The coaches laugh and chat away at trackside. Six of them on a wooden bench. A caretaker is cutting the football pitch with an old-fashioned lawnmower. Back and forth, back and forth in the tall grass. The sweat is pouring down his bare chest. The colour is starting to flake from the stadium's white concrete terraces.

The athletes run interval after interval. It's the middle of the day and the sun makes the air shimmer. After an interval, one of the athletes runs over to his clothes for a drink of water. One of the trainers runs across at once and hits him with a stick.

'No water!'

The runner sprints away. The other trainers laugh. The one who got hit across the back is one of the best, he has won big races all over the world. On the running track, everyone is treated the same.

After the training, Zakharias buys three Fantas for Naftal, Dominic and myself. That sweet orange taste in a glass bottle. Fantastic.

WE ARE DOING DISTANCE RUNNING and I am in the middle of the pack. There's a distinct acceleration with every uphill section.

I am on the right side of the limit, no lactic acid. I am running with the blood, with the oxygen. I can just keep on running for as long as it takes.

I've lost six kilos since I've been here. If I only carry on cutting down on food, I'm sure I can lose a few more kilos.

During the training when the blood circulates quickly, I don't feel hungry. The energy then seems to come from somewhere far inside the body, like the bone marrow. I only think about the breathing and I disconnect my body from my head. There is nothing else.

It's starting to rain, heavy drops that come down from the sky with astonishing force. There's a sudden panic within the group.

'Markos, we can't stay out in the rain,' says Naftal. 'Something comes up out of the ground that makes us ill. We have to find some shelter.'

We pass a hut with a tin roof and everyone runs across to it. There we stand, tightly packed, while the rain hammers against the roof. I don't get it. I would prefer to be out in the rain and to feel the heavy, cool drops on my head. I ask Naftal what it is that comes out of the ground.

'I don't know, but you get sick.'

Then it's all calm again. The rain has gone away as fast as it came. The sun comes out and we carry on running along the muddy paths. The others are really bad when it comes to running on a slippery surface, and now they are the ones that haven't a hope of keeping up with my pace.

I come back home all muddy, shower, rinse off my shoes and wash my socks. I eat a ripe mango and drink my corn gruel. I go down to the medical hut to get the result of the test that I left there a few days earlier. My stomach feels weird and I'm exhausted.

The doctor is wearing glasses and has got nice, gentle hands.

'Markos,' he says. 'No malaria, no typhoid. That is good. But you have amoeba and hookworm in your stomach. Not dangerous, but you need to take some medicine. If you get a temperature you must come back.'

I wander back alone through the village. People are smiling at me from every house that I pass. Everyone recognises me. Some children are following me along the narrow pathways. Barefoot on muddy paths, is this how the Messiah felt?

When I get back home there's food waiting for me on the table. Mama Gwandu has made dagaar, tiny salted dried fish, which she buys in big bags in the market at Arusha. She fries them with tomato and garlic. The tastes explode in my head. There and then it tastes like the nicest thing I've ever eaten.

WE ARE GOING TO BE RUNNING INTERVALS on the coffee fields and we jog there from home at about nine in the morning. We will run along the foot of the mountain, no hills, all on the flat. I feel a little short of energy. We cross the road that goes to Kenya and reach the fields just under an hour later.

Zakharias is waiting for us in the shade of a low tree. I'm feeling wobbly. I'm longing for a hole in the ice so I could dive down into the darkness and the cold. I'm incredibly hungry.

We set off – we run fast for three or four minutes and jog for a while to recover. I'm now on the wrong side of the limit. The lactic acid is making my legs sore. My body hasn't time to recover between the intervals. I slip behind, and lack the energy to focus. The training ends after an eternity.

'Markos, tired today?' asks Zakharias.

'Yup, my legs are slow today.'

Naftal laughs when he sees me.

'Markos, no problem.'

Zakharias walks along with us when we make our way home. He knocks on the door of a wrinkled little farmer, hands over some money and buys 30 centimetres of sugar cane for each of us.

An orgasm in the mouth. The energy kicks in and makes me feel like the Hulk. The sugar cane is sharp and cuts my lips, but I keep on chewing until I've sucked out every ounce of sugar.

ONE NIGHT I DREAM ABOUT MUM. In the dream she's driving her electric wheelchair with shaking hands. She's down at the port and drives on to the quay, right up to the edge. She's been secured to the chair with her seat belt. Then she goes too close and topples into the sea, flying like the bicycle in *E.T.* through the air and into the cold water.

She can't free herself and sinks deeper and deeper. The air is pushed out of her lungs.

She gets smaller and smaller until she reaches the bottom 15 metres down. The wheelchair sinks down into the mud.

No greenery. No seaweed. Just darkness.

I should be there.

MAMA GWANDU'S SISTER'S HUSBAND HAS DIED. Zakharias says that he died of AIDS, or was it pneumonia? In any case, he coughed a lot towards the end.

The sister receives us with tears in her eyes. It's the first time I've met her and it feels like a weird encounter. The women go out into the kitchen and the rest of us sit down at the table, in the middle of which is a big round bowl filled with food. We eat chicken and fried rice with our hands straight from the bowl.

The men around the table speak Swahili. I understand a bit, but I haven't made a real effort to learn it properly. I have focused on just running and resting. All my energy goes to my body.

I'm surrounded by people but alone with my own thoughts. It's like a Christmas party and a wake rolled into one. Not much separates them really. Presents, food, hunger and a man who died from AIDS.

It's different here. Death and grief are faced in a different way.

I'M SQUATTING BEHIND A SHRUB, taking a shit. The others are running on. They know that I can find my home on my own nowadays. It's the amoeba that is playing up. A gnawing pain in my stomach, which comes and goes. My shit smells of egg. I wipe myself with green leaves and prickly grass and run on.

Good to run on my own for a bit. I miss that. I am longing to be tucked into a sleeping bag again, with a cold nose and smoking breath that is sucked up through the hole at the top of my tent. I run into a tree and scratch my thigh. Damn it!

I pull down my trousers, pee into my hand and wash my scratch with dark urine. I've got an enormous respect for small cuts. Just as well to clean it straight away.

After a while, I catch up with Patrick, who has also fallen behind. We push ourselves to catch up with the others. Patrick has missed training for a few days. He's been feeling weak and has been taking medicines against malaria, typhoid, hookworm and amoeba. His eyes are tired. He's probably still running a temperature.

We catch up with the others and I place myself at the back of the pack. They are running faster, but I keep up. Patrick looks floppy, his hips and legs don't seem synchronised. He falls back while the rest of us carry on up the mountain.

The treeline here is much higher than in Jämtland. Permanent greenery, no obvious contrasts. Everything is growing at a phenomenal rate: a light green straw today, a banana tree tomorrow.

Naftal is applying the pressure and I am focused on his back in front of me. I imagine that I am attached to it with a strong rubber band. We reach one more plateau before we turn around at last and start running downhill. Great not to need to focus any more, now I can just keep rolling.

Back home I finish off with 150 sit-ups and 50 press-ups. The power in my arms is gone. They are as thin as two sticks.

I've lost eight kilos in four months. And I will never be the best.

I see the ease with which my friends flow along, and to compare myself with them feels almost ridiculous. They have got relaxed legs and strong glutes; they're thin and explosive at the same time. However much I train, I will never be able to run like them.

My body is not adjusted to running. I have bigger calves and more muscles and I'm heftier right across the board.

My head loves running. I am a runner. I can see myself running 10 kilometres in 28 minutes if everything is optimal. Any faster than that just won't happen. It's simply not within me.

For that, I would have to be reborn in a different body.

ONE DAY WE TAKE AN EARLY morning taxi far out onto the savannah. I'm wearing my knitted hat and coveralls. Outside it's dark and cold. We're packed like sardines on the back seat. We are going to be dropped off 35 kilometres from home. There's not another living soul as far as the eye can see.

We start running back home. After a while, we go past a lonely shepherd who is standing wrapped up in a blanket by the side of the road. A bit further away, there are some really scrawny cows. The shepherd has a wooden club in his hand as protection against predators.

I think that I could have exchanged lives with him and been quite contented. My cows, a wooden club and a lion. Up to me to defend the animals that are providing my food.

The sun rises and burns away the morning dew. The day is getting warm. We run calmly, about four minutes per kilometre. The closer we get to Arusha, the more there is of everything: people, smells, houses and cars. The black asphalt is burning beneath our feet.

We are overtaken by a truck that is pulling along a cyclist holding firmly to the back of the truck with his right hand. The driver is going fast, probably about 70 kilometres per hour. The cyclist is going along with one hand on the handlebar. He looks happy and relaxed. A bit further on the driver stops dead at a crossing. The cyclist loses his grip and carries on straight over the crossing and collides head-on with another truck.

When we run past, the cyclist is completely crushed. His head is flattened, his body twisted. He no longer looks like a human being. On the truck we can see blood and splintered bones. I wonder what he was thinking. It all happened so quickly. People come rushing up, they pull away the bike and drag away the corpse. We carry on running. The blood is pounding away in my temples.

When we get home, I peel a green orange and drink some warm water. Did I really see someone being crushed 45 minutes ago? It feels unreal to be standing here eating a sweet orange.

Everything happens so quickly here. The sun rises in one minute and sets just as quickly. The line between life and death is thinner here. I am pining for a long, slow twilight, which I have time to take in.

BOHUSLÄN CHEESECAKE, SMOKED SALMON and Jansson's temptation. And cider. I'm dying for some cider. For the fizz and sweet taste in my mouth.

I know that everything will be fucked up if I don't start eating more. I weigh 53 kilos and I can see the outline of every bone through my skin. I've crossed some kind of threshold. I think about food all the time.

The last ounce of my energy is starting to disappear, but I don't manage to break free from this spiral. Every time I eat, a sense of panic rises inside of me. My head keeps pushing me: you must get thinner, Markus, if you want to run faster.

I feel totally fucked.

I really can't get any thinner than I am right now. If I do, I won't be able to run at all. My body will have worked its way through its fat reserves, and if I don't fill up with some more energy, it will just stop working.

My thoughts move slowly as well. Lacking anything else, my body has probably started to eat up the fat in my brain. Why do I have to go to such extremes? To overdo everything?

My body and my brain have separate wills that fight over the same space.

I'm looking through the journal that I write in every day. Every sentence starts with, I, I, I . . .

ONE SATURDAY EVENING Dam-Dam and I are walking along the dark roads between the houses. We are on our way to the farmer to buy milk. Once a week, we make milky tea. Zakharias says that our lungs will get heavy if we drink it more often.

The farmer has one lonely cow. It is white and bony and I can't understand how she can produce any milk at all. She looks so dry and thirsty. We buy two litres and go back with the fresh, warm milk in a battered tin bucket. We make a fire, boil up the milk and add the finely ground black tea leaves. We let it brew for a while before pouring it into big cups.

Naftal, Dam-Dam, Dominic, Zakharias and I are sitting out there in the darkness below the trees, drinking the tea in short gulps. I sprinkle many spoonfuls of sugar into my cup. All I can see of the others is the whites of their eyes. Nobody says anything. The mosquitoes are whining.

Zakharias says that Naftal and Dam-Dam have children. Naftal has a daughter who's a year old. Dam-Dam has four children and a wife who live in a nearby village just a few kilometres away. They don't see their families very often, only a couple of times a year – before and after the running season.

They don't get to see their children growing up. Instead, they use their most productive years to make money. It was the same for Grandad. He was at home when one of his four children was born, but for the others he was out at sea. I spent more time with Grandad than Mum did.

I drink the fat-rich milk, aware of the milk proteins spreading out through my blood, repairing my torn muscle fibres. I can't see any moon, only tiny stars far away in the sky. This is the high point of the week.

MY SIX MONTHS HAVE PASSED. I long for cold rain and dark forests. And for being on my own with my own plate.

My speech is slow, the pathways of the nerves from my brain to my mouth don't seem to be working too well. I sound like Mum when she's tired.

I give away all my training clothes. Patrick gets a pair of my worn-out shoes. They are too big for him, but his own shoes are falling apart, so he prefers mine. The second pair I throw away – they are just too far gone. My light blue running shorts I give to Dominic. They are still just about holding together, just a little hole in the crotch. Dam-Dam gets my long tights so that he can run without making that rustling noise. Naftal gets my thick cotton sweater and my purple running vest with the crest of Duved's athletics club on it. Zakharias gets my woolly underwear and my anorak. I give a pair of socks each to Dominic, Naftal and Dam-Dam. Patrick gets the spare pair of long johns.

I walk down to the miller because I'm planning to carry on with the gruel when I get back home. He removes the bran and grinds the corn into a fine powder that looks like Graham flour. I pack it into double bags, which I carry on my back. I barely have the strength to get the flour back to the house. Thirty kilos weighs more now than it did four months ago.

When I get back to the house, Mama Gwandu has prepared a chicken. My favourite dish. I eat more than I usually do and at once I feel stressed inside. I say thanks for the food and give everybody a big hug straight from my heart. A quick finish. Like a quick sunrise or a head-on collision with a lorry. Their kind expressions stay with me as I go back inside to pack up the few things that I am not leaving behind.

I put on the CD player and lie down on my bed. I listen to 'Lullaby' by Low and wait for the dawn.

The others are asleep when I get up. I walk alone through the dark down to the bus station. I can see no shining eyes looking back at me through the darkness, no children are running up to me. The flour in my rucksack is assuming the shape of my back. Now I just want to get home.

I sit on the bus for the whole day. We pass giraffes and elephants. It's like travelling across the sea, you can see so far in every direction. No trees, just green grass and the animals and the odd Masai with a red blanket over his shoulder and a wooden club in his hand.

We arrive at the airport in Nairobi in the evening. Two hours before the plane leaves, and I'm trying to find where to check in. I'm starving and tired and I am desperate to sink into my seat on the plane. I can't find my flight on the information board and I have an odd feeling like a little bird fluttering in my chest. Bloody hell. Why does everything always go wrong?

I can't cope with any more problems. I examine my ticket, but everything seems OK.

I find someone by one of the gates and ask if he has heard anything about my plane. He looks at me intently and says that there's no such flight this evening.

'But I have a ticket for the plane tonight,' I protest.

'Can I see it?'

He takes a quick look.

'It went yesterday.'

'Are you kidding?'

'No, I'm not. You misread your ticket. You are landing in Gothenburg on the seventh, which is today. The flight left yesterday.'

'So what am I going to do now, then?'

'I don't know,' the man answers brusquely.

I feel like punching him in the nose, but I don't. After all, it's not his fault. You're up shit creek, Torgeby.

I lie down on a bench and try to breathe deeply. Most of all I want to go to the toilet and flush myself down the pipes and float all the way out to sea. I have 100 kronor [$12] in my pocket and no ticket. What do I do now?

I change the last of my money so that at least I can buy some food. I make my way out of the terminal and find a place that sells beans and corn gruel. I concentrate on the food and on nothing else. I feel good. My brain is starting to work again. I have some coins. Perhaps I can phone someone? The travel agency, didn't they have a helpline?

I go back in and phone Kilroy Travels and spin them a yarn about riots, a driver who had a heart attack and petrol that ran out. They book me onto the next flight to Sweden.

Hallelujah.

AT LANDVETTER, DAD GREETS ME with open arms. We take the motorway towards Gothenburg past road signs with white text on a blue background. Wonderful to be home. We pass Landvetter cemetery, where the Boxer is buried. It is four years since I carried the coffin, but I can still feel the weight on my shoulder. I think about him every day and wonder why I am still alive while he is being consumed by the earth. I think about death a lot, about it getting closer all the time.

Dad puts his warm hand over mine. He always does this when we're driving. Driving always works fine for us. There's no anger when we're in the car together. It's our time.

We drive onto the ferry and I step outside and go up to the railings at the ship's prow. It is chilly outside and it feels so good to be a bit cold. I see the port of Öckerö and the big crane by the wharf. All is calm and still. I breathe in the salty, damp air. I haven't spoken to anyone in Sweden for six months. I've just been in my own bubble.

I wonder what would happen if I fell into the water in front of the ferry. Would I manage to swim below it? On this particular day I don't think I would have managed.

MUM IS ASLEEP ON THE SOFA when I get home. The same sofa as before but now covered in black material. The same Carola on the CD player. My little sister Ida is at home and says that I look completely weird.

'You look like a walking stickman with two sunken eyes.'

'Surely it's not that bad,' I say.

'Yes, it is. A mixture of a concentration camp and Biafra children.'

Grandma and Grandad come in.

'Good God, what has happened, Markus?' says Grandma. 'What have you been doing down there in Africa?'

'Running,' I answer.

I make some corn gruel on the cooker. I haven't eaten since I left Nairobi. The food on the plane looked strange, so I gave it a miss.

'What sort of rubbish are you making?' wonders Grandma.

'Corn gruel.'

'Corn gruel? What's wrong with potatoes?'

'Nothing, but corn gruel is great. Everyone in Africa lives on it.'

'I'm sure they do, and no wonder they are all so small.'

MY SISTER IDA AND I ARE STROLLING AROUND on the island. I'm wrapped up in several layers of clothes and have pulled my knitted hat down over my ears. My joints feel stiff. It's as if my body has run out of lubrication.

I say hi to the people that I recognise. It seems to me that everyone looks so big and pale, like giants. I panic when I see all the white flesh walking past. I think of all the food that must be eaten to maintain such enormous bodies. Ida complains: 'What's up with you, Markus? Just because you look like a skeleton, you don't have to walk like one.'

'What do you mean? I'm not walking slowly. I've always walked like this.'

'Come off it. You move like a snail.'

We're walking past the light-coloured reeds by Rördammen, over the heather and the rocks down towards the sea. A westerly wind is blowing and the waves are foaming. I haven't felt a a cool wind on my face for ages.

ONE DAY, I STEP ONTO Mum's scales. 52.2 kilos. I've lost 12 kilos in six months.

It feels weird inside. I feel no life, no strength. I know that I have to start to eat, but my head still says no. It doesn't matter that Ida and Grandma say that I look like a skeleton; I still have a feeling of anxiety for every mouthful that I swallow.

How can this be? What does it matter whether I run 10 kilometres in 31 or 28 minutes?

I look at my own reflection and see a body that can surely become even lighter. I am absolutely certain of that. It's almost like something chemical or physical in my head, like a watertight compartment between this thought and everything else. I am standing in the darkness at the bottom of a well and I see the freedom and the food up there, but the walls are slippery and I can't climb up.

When my thought process works so slowly, the thoughts that do come are big ones.

Why am I doing all this?

The only time that life seems easy is when I am on my own.

I AM LYING NEXT TO MUM on the sofa. She is incredibly tired. She speaks slowly in short sentences. She says nothing about the curtains, she isn't even crying any more. I think she has run out of tears.

'Markus, do you think that I will get well again?'

'I hope so, but I don't know,' I say.

She looks at me with her blue eyes.

'My body feels like a heavy stone,' she says. 'I'm so tired of lying here.'

'I get that,' I say. 'But you're doing well.'

If it was me lying there with a body that doesn't respond, I would have gone down to the port with my pockets stuffed with rocks. I would have exhaled all the air on my way down to the bottom and taken a deep breath, filling my lungs with salt water. And woken up among the angels or the devils.

This is something that I have thought many times, it's a terror that I carry around deep inside my head.

'Do you have to go away so soon?' says Mum. 'You've only been home two weeks.'

'There's no space for me here.'

'Don't say that. You're my boy and you can be here as much as you like.'

'Mum, I need to be on my own for a bit. I'm tired in my body and in my head. I am longing for the forest.'

I give her a hug and say cheerio. It's time.

Dad puts his hand over mine as he drives me down to the ferry.

GOING BACK

I'M WATCHING THE RED REAR LIGHTS of the train disappearing down the valley towards Storlien. I am the only one getting off at Undersåker. The station lies abandoned.

The sun is shining from a clear blue sky and I breathe in the dry air. It is a few degrees colder than on Öckerö. There's still snow above the treeline, otherwise the ground is bare. The birches are beginning to bud; spring is on its way.

At ICA I buy fruit, raisins, a really big load of porridge oats, and tinned mackerel in tomato sauce. I don't run into anyone I know as I trudge up the long hill towards the E14; there's no one to say hi to. It feels good to be alone. I decide not to hitch-hike, so I walk the five kilometres to Hålland.

I sneak into the college. The code on the lock to the storeroom is the same as before I went to Tanzania. My sleeping bags, the camping stove, and the reindeer hides are still in the hiding place in the corner, next to the plastic box with the cotton sheet for the tent. I hoist it all up on my back and start walking.

The rucksack is digging into my shoulders as I walk over the hill. I feel scarily weak, as if my arms aren't properly attached. My feet get wet as I ford the Slagsån.

Six months have passed since I was last in the clearing, and nature has begun to reclaim it. The horsehair mattress is soaked and birds and voles have gnawed holes in the fabric, but the bed itself is basically OK. I put it back in the place it was before I left, unroll two reindeer hides, take out the sleeping bag and lie down on my back. The sky is still blue. It's 8°C. I close my eyes and wake up many hours later, my body heavy and relaxed.

The tomato sauce splashes onto my sweater when I open a tin of mackerel. My whole body smells of old fish as I walk down to the stream for a drink. The ice-cold water gives me a brief brain freeze, but God, how I have longed for this over the past few months – to drink pure, cold water without having to worry about amoebas and typhoid.

The black garbage bag is still hanging under the fir tree. The axe, the saw, my spices, my work trousers, my boots, everything has survived, even though the axe is a little rusty.

I've decided to change living quarters. On the south side of Helgesjön, there is a little clearing surrounded in all directions by really dense forest and very hard to find. There are more birches here and the ground is wetter. The moss will make it gentler on the legs.

It's only about a kilometre to the new place and I pack up as much as I can manage before starting out. My heart beats slowly, my body feels sluggish and feeble. It's frustrating to be so bloody weak. I have to take five trips before I have collected all the equipment, the bed and the 20 poles. I leave the horsehair mattress behind for nature to take its course.

I tie up the tripod and erect the skeleton of the tent, which settles nicely into the moss and the grass. I cover it with the canvas, and collect some stones from the edge of the lake to support the bed. There is a faint smell of smoke from the cloth; I inhale it through my nose and draw it down into my lungs. I hear the ice creaking and cracking on the lake. I collect another lot of stones to build the fireplace, and I test it to make sure the smoke goes where it should. This is going to be fine.

With dusk comes the cold and I have to collect firewood. Luckily there's plenty of dead, dry fir trees nearby. The fir needles get caught in my hat and my green woollen sweater as I drag the branches through the forest. The inside of my arms are smarting from the scratches of the day's slog.

But with the fire going I can sink down into the bed. Memories. This is my home, and here I do what I like.

THE NEXT MORNING, I GET UP EARLY and change into running gear. I run over the night frost, my legs stiff. My ankles hurt every time I have to accommodate a root or make a sudden movement. My joints have lost their elasticity.

I go for a gentle distance-run along the Indalsälven past the Ristafallet and Åkroken and then uphill to Norsjön, where the ice is still intact. Kilometre after kilometre alone across the vast open spaces.

Back home I wash in the zero-degree water of Helgesjön's outflow. My whole body is freezing.

Inside the tent I put on dry clothes, and dry my hair in front of the fire. This is something I have been missing as well.

ONE DAY BERTIL PICKS ME UP in his silver Mercedes. We are going to Strömsund up in the very north of Jämtland, where I am to run a 10-kilometre race on asphalt.

My legs feel incredibly stiff. I am still cutting down on food, although I realise that this can't go on. My hands are cold all the time and my lips are purple.

Bertil is in a good mood and tells me that he has done a lot of skiing in the winter, a short distance every day in the Duved track. His hair is still dark although he has been retired for a few years. Bertil was born in Härjedalen and is more interested in sport than in hunting. He played football with Tord Grip [the former coach and manager] when he was young.

Bertil wants to know if I have got enough firewood stored and how my mum is getting on. I tell him about Tanzania and he wants to know how we managed our training there – lengths, times, speeds. After three hours, we arrive in a cold and windy Strömsund. Spring has taken a few backward steps.

The race will go twice around a five-kilometre course and I begin my warm-up 50 minutes before the start. I jog once round the track and feel the stiffness disappear. I do some stops and starts before changing into my running shoes, my long tights and top. The race starts and I'm off.

I'm alone in the lead. I hardly breathe. I run the first kilometre in 2 minutes 50 seconds. After two kilometres I slow down and run the last eight kilometres at a relaxed pace. My winning time is 31 minutes, several minutes before the second place runner. Everything feels meaningless. Why am I competing? Why travel 500 kilometres there and back to run 10 kilometres on asphalt?

I wind down by running another lap, shower and put on dry clothes. I get into the car and eat a pear. Bertil turns up the heating and we set off for home.

'Do you need something else to eat?' he wonders.

'That's OK,' I say. 'I'll have something when I get home.'

'You run well, Markus. You are light and quick, you flow.'

Then he falls silent. I feel that he has something else to say, that he has picked up on the battle I am fighting within myself. But he doesn't say anything. I think he understands that it wouldn't do any good. I am inside my bubble and must pierce a hole in it myself.

I jump out at Hållandsgården and start walking. My legs ache. It feels as if there's gravel inside my knees.

THEN SPRING REALLY COMES. Everything starts growing and the birds fall silent only for a few hours when the night is at its darkest. My sleeping is still weird, and I wake every morning feeling tired, my face swollen. There is something happening deep within me that I can't quite reach. It's whirring away and doesn't give me any peace at night.

I collect the new leaves from the birches until I am fed up with the bitter taste. My tongue goes green and looks like that of a cow. I chop off a birch branch instead and attach a bottle to it to collect the sap because I have heard it contains a lot of vitamins and minerals. Some hours later, the bottle is full. The sap is sweet like a very diluted, still bottle of pop and I drink it down in huge gulps.

I can't walk around any longer like a hollow-eyed stickman. I want to inhabit my body and see the forest and know myself. I want to be free. I don't want to waste energy thinking about what not to eat. I will never open that door again.

I start eating. There is plenty of resistance in my brain, but I tell my head to bugger off. I force myself to change direction. I make myself eat porridge, fruit and nuts and experience a mix of anxiety and pleasure. Eating gets easier with every mouthful I swallow. Like filling up a bottomless hole.

I AM DOING SOME WHITTLING, sitting on the chopping block inside the tent, quite near the opening, my belly full of breakfast porridge. The sun shines in and warms my face. The fire is about to go out.

I peel off the thin, soft bark from a fresh stick of birch wood until I reach the white flesh. It smells good and feels soft against my fingers. I peel the whole stick clean.

Then I hear a strange sound behind me, like sandpaper dragged across cotton. I look over my shoulder and see how the canvas of the tent is pressed down by a thick tongue. I stop whittling and sit completely still like a dead fir tree.

The elk comes close to the opening. I feel it but don't dare to turn around. My eyes are wide open. I can't blink. I breathe slowly.

Finally it comes around to the opening. It has to turn its head to accommodate its horns. I am 30 centimetres from his nose. I see the moist brown muzzle with its little warts. I feel his warm breath. The elk doesn't see me.

At last I raise my arm very slowly and say, 'Hi.'

No reaction.

'How's it going?' I say. 'You're a bit close.'

Then the elk jumps backwards, about three metres or so. It stops and looks at me for a moment before turning round and rushing off. As it disappears into the forest, his legs remind me of the African runners – narrow and light just above the foot. Explosive but capable of sustained effort.

Now I'm back. The forest has let me in.

MY MONEY IS STARTING TO RUN OUT. I've got only a few hundred kronor left in my account. In Järpen there is an old people's home and one day I track down the manager on my way home from the shop. She tells me that there's always work there.

A week or so later, I get up at 5.45 and run the 11 kilometres along the E14 to Järpen. I am doing the same jobs that I did with Mum: caring, washing bums, putting cream on dry feet, doling out medicine and talking to people about the past. That's the fun part of the job, to hear stories from long ago when the old people remember elk hunts, encounters with bears, the autumn harvest, and how they stood in the late summer sunshine, working in the hay with sweaty backs.

At lunchtime I go down to the shop and buy some black pudding, which I fry in the kitchen of the home. I fill my stomach with blood and flour and drink the tap water.

I am managing on my own; it would never occur to me to live off benefits. But it feels hard to be walking around the corridors when the sun is shining outdoors. I don't understand how people can work every day. Myself, my body starts getting heavy like a physical depression, the same feeling as when Mum asked me to close the curtains.

I can run 100 kilometres without food, but already in the first day at this job I am seized by panic. I don't understand how this can happen. I feel spoiled for being so weak and not managing what most people can do without any problem.

The old people deserve someone better than me.

After work, I run past Norsjön on the way home. I go past some wonderful old fir trees and can see Åreskutan in the distance. I run off the heaviness in my legs and bathe myself clean in Helgesjön.

I manage five days in the nursing home and then I have enough money for three months.

I START SLEEPING PROPERLY AGAIN – deep and dreamless sleep. I go to bed early even if the sun is still high in the sky, and wake up relaxed and rested the following day. My body is regaining all the lost sleep.

For every day that I carry on eating, my thoughts are getting quicker and not so heavy. Time is starting to move faster. And my muscles are beginning to strengthen. My heart can't keep up as my body grows, and the running is more of an effort. I have more weight to drag around, but I don't care.

I debate with myself as if I am two different people. I ask questions and try to find answers. *Why do I go to such lengths? What is it that makes my body calm when I push myself, when I am really cold or am a little hungry?*

Questions without answers, but they don't concern anyone but me.

When the summer comes, I begin to read *Sayings of the Desert Fathers*. I was given the book by a college friend a few years ago, and it has been hanging in a bag on the clothes line in the tent. Now I feel like having a look.

The book is about the first Christian monks who moved out into the Egyptian desert a few years after Jesus's death. They lived like hermits on water and bread. They lived in caves and holes in the ground, without meeting anyone. They looked at life with different eyes, far removed from achievement and status. They wrote about a God that I can believe in, a God who is fair and not judgemental. Who understands that it is not easy to be a human being.

I read the 2000-year-old words and recognise myself in the monks' thoughts and words. They write about doubt, about living in one world at a time. Nothing high-falutin', but simple words from simple people. Antonius, one of these first monks, writes: 'There will come a time when people are mad and if they meet someone who isn't mad, they'll turn to him and say, "You are mad", because he isn't like them.'

I read two pages a day throughout the whole summer. The monks live like me, although even harder: less food, water and sleep, and heavier work.

I read, eat and run. The running helps me get the words into my chest. I run across the marshes and hills. 'God is not in the strength but the truth.' I think that this is exactly what preoccupies me – I am looking for the truth about myself by being silent.

Perhaps I should become a monk? Move far out into the Alaskan wilderness, staking my life, to see where I end up. I am at a crossroads, I can feel that clearly. If I carry on along the road I have chosen, I will never be able to return to ordinary life again.

I GET UP EARLY AND START RUNNING TOWARDS Vålådalen. The morning is cold and clear. When I pass the shop in Undersåker I buy a couple of Snickers, and then I carry on along the asphalt road towards the mountains. Along the horizon the mountain tops are soft and white with frost. I want to run up all of them.

I run in long tights and a thin top, wear a woolly hat and an anorak tied around my waist. It is early autumn and the colours are starting to come. Red leaves where the frost has been, otherwise mostly yellow.

I run past the road to Ottsjö, and on towards Fångemon and Valbo. Fir trees and little mountain birch trees on both sides of the road. The sun starts to warm the back of my neck. I drink the water from Vålån and carry on down into the valley.

This is where Gunder Hägg lived and trained. He was the world's best runner in the 1940s, the years when he was at his peak. I run past the marsh that bears his name and come to the mountain lodge. I have run 35 kilometres at a slow pace and still feel good, a little tight around the knees perhaps – the soles of my shoes are hard-worn after all those miles run.

I go into the red building, drink a little more water and eat both Snickers. The energy goes straight into my blood. I sit down outside on a wooden bench with the sun on my face.

A bit further off there is a running track and a sports hall. Some of the world's best athletes – in skiing, skating and running – trained here during the decades after Gunder's glory days, up until the 1990s. Here they built up their basic fitness in the gentle, rolling terrain. In the winter they skated around Nultjärn or skied up the Ottfjället; in the summer they ran across the marshes and the mountain slopes. It must have been exotic for the foreign athletes to train in the summer sun that never sets, with the mountains and the clear air all around.

I stretch my thighs and start the homeward run. The energy lasts for 20 kilometres, then it gets tough. I long for some food, my thoughts shrink – I can't see the mountains any more, just the asphalt road in front of my feet. I want to lie down in the grass and have a rest, but I carry on. I become unsteady and slow, my muscles are tired; it feels as if I am running just with my skeleton. But my heart doesn't feel any effort.

The memories from hungry runs in Tanzania spring to life, but now I am on my own and don't need to worry about anyone else.

It is just up to me to get myself back home. I roll down the eight kilometres from Trillevallen to Undersåker. In the shop I buy an apple drink and two bananas. It is worth a little bit of hunger to properly enjoy a banana and some apple juice.

I run the last seven kilometres home, over Romohöjden and the marsh above the Slagsån. I come down to Helgesjön, longing for a big helping of porridge with a thick layer of honey on top. When I have had a wash, I warm up by the fire and stuff myself with the food.

Then I lie in bed, tend the fire and drink warm tea until the colour of my pee goes from dark orange to light yellow.

THE FIRST SNOW IS FALLING and forms a skin over the tent. I hit the canvas so that the snow slides off and forms an insulating wall at ground level. No cold wind can come through to my bed any longer. My home will be drier and warmer. The forest will be lighter. Life will be easier.

When I go outside one morning, I see big, round lynx tracks around the tent. It's a powerful feeling to know that I was lying down, asleep so close by. The big cat with the pointed ears must have felt that I was in there behind the canvas and have heard my breathing. I imagine that it stopped and listened for a moment before silently sloping off.

ONE DAY AN OLD MATE FROM COLLEGE, Stig-Mikael, returns to Hålland. We used to talk about making a long skiing trip together. Now we decide that it would be fun to ski along the whole Swedish mountain range, 1300 kilometres from Grövelsjön in the south to Treriksröset in the north.

We talk about how long it would take and what sort of equipment we'll be needing. Before he goes back to Norway, it's all settled. This is going to happen.

Now I really need money and the old people's home really need help. I need to work for six weeks. I'll ski down in the mornings and do what has to be done and ski back home again. After four weeks I just want to cry, but I have got this goal, so I just have to bite the bullet.

In early February, Stig-Mikael is back. We shop around for all the equipment and borrow our mate Jocke's kitchen, where we bake energy biscuits. We mix up a lot of oats, eggs, chocolate and butter, which we bake in the oven and then cut up into pieces that we put into plastic bags. We make up four big packages, and send these by coach to the places along the mountain range where there are people who agree to hold onto our food: Storliens boarding house, the tourist bureau in Gäddede, the youth hostel in Tärnaby and Abisko mountain lodge.

On 14 February, the preparations are done and we catch the bus heading south.

WE SLEEP ONE NIGHT at the Grövelsjön mountain lodge and set out early the next morning. We ski the route northwards and simply follow the red crosses marking the way. A fantastic feeling to get started and just glide across the snow, everything I need in the sledge behind me: two bedmats, the winter sleeping bag, a windproof bag; head torch, ski skins and wax; a plastic bottle, two one-litre thermoses, cutlery; spare socks, a thick woollen sweater, camping socks, woollen mittens and thin cotton inner mittens. On my upper body I have a woollen string vest and a cotton anorak; on my legs cotton trousers and snowgaiters. Not a fantastic amount of clothes – it's the moving that will keep us warm.

I have the tent on my sledge, and Mikael has the camping stove on his. The fuel and the food we have shared between us so that we pull equal loads.

Everything is simple: ski, eat and sleep. The same routine, day after day.

In the mornings we take turns getting up first while the other one can sleep in. The thing is to melt enough snow – at least seven litres are needed to make the breakfast porridge and fill the water bottles and thermoses for the day. After an hour or so, the morning task has been done and we have breakfast together. Then we take down the tent and move on, 25–30 kilometres a day.

We take two food breaks a day, the first around 11 o'clock and the second around 2, when we nibble on energy biscuits and drink warm soup. Towards the evening we find sheltered places below the treeline, where we put up the tent and cover it with snow. With the camp kitchen between us inside the warm tent, we prepare dinner together. In the evenings it will be protein: freeze-dried dishes, preserved tuna. Then we draw on the map how far we have skied that day and chat until we fall asleep.

I am reading Kerstin Ekman's *Blackwater*, a scary book about a murder in a tent, which takes place at Valsjöbyn, not far from here. The whole book is steeped in a sense of unease.

After some days we pass Vemdalen and then turn north past Sylarna, up towards my home territory. We go past Storlien and carry on towards Valsjöbyn. The dry cold turns into warmer weather and rain. The going is becoming heavy, the snow feels like porridge under the skis.

When we get to Valsjöbyn, we are soaked to the skin and everything feels miserable. We go into the store and buy some sweets. Once inside, in the stagnant atmosphere, I can sense that I smell of sweat. We ask the girl if there is any youth hostel open because we need to dry our stuff and I am desperate for a warm bath, but we are told that everything is closed. Then a woman standing next to us says that we can stay a night with her. She's called Lena and lives above the shop. Wonderful!

We pick up all our wet clothes and go upstairs to Lena's flat. She's about 50 and tells us that she's a hairdresser. There's something odd about her, which I can't quite put my finger on. She's just not quite all there. But she gives us Norway's national dish – lamb and cabbage stew. It's good to eat at the table instead of in a sleeping bag.

When Stig-Mikael and I are about to go up to her attic and to bed, she asks him if he wouldn't like to stay and have a bit of a 'cosy time' with her. He thanks her for the offer but declines.

I feel a bit of a shiver down my spine when we go upstairs. Stig-Mikael feels just as uncomfortable and he finds a heavy vase, which he puts next to himself before he gets into his sleeping bag to use as a weapon in case Lena turns up in the night. I can't stop thinking about *Blackwater*. All through the night I'm tense and am quite convinced that Lena is going to jump in with a long knife and slice up my stomach. Neither of us can sleep a wink.

Next morning we get up early, collect our stuff and sneak downstairs. Lena is nowhere to be seen. We tiptoe out through the door, put on our skis and head off as fast as we can.

We ski on. Jämtland becomes Västerbotten, we reach Vindel-fjällen in south Lappland and carry on towards Padjelanta. We ski over hills with endless views in all directions, we see wolverine tracks and elks running in a line across the mountain. The weather is mild and very windy.

When we come up to Padjelanta, the wind coming across the mountain is so strong that we cannot go any further. We find a hut that gives us shelter, and we put up the tent behind it. There we remain marooned by the wind for several days. We can barely put a foot outside. The only thing we can do is stay inside the tent and talk.

When the wind dies down we move on, our backs stiff after three days' rest. The whole vast landscape is covered in fresh snow, and dragging the sledge is like pulling a heavy plough.

In the evening the wind picks up again and we search out one of the province's unmanned mountain huts. In the middle of the night, we are woken up by a couple of Sami carrying a third who is so drunk that he can't talk and looks in a bad way. They have been in Gällivare getting drunk and are now driving home across the mountain by scooter.

'Per-Åke,' they shout to their semi-conscious friend. 'You better stay here for a bit.'

And to us: 'We lost Jon on the mountain. He fell off somewhere. We have to turn round and find him.'

Then they disappear. Per-Åke is rambling, so we can't really get any sleep. He keeps coming up with incomprehensible outbursts. In the morning he is fast asleep when we leave the hut. His scooter stands in a snowdrift outside. There's no sign of Jon and the others. The wind has died down again and we head off.

We ski into the Sarek national park from the west and go through the valley between the mountains that remind me of Sylarna, through they're a bit steeper and sharper. We carry on between the hills and can see Kebnekaise in the distance.

The days are longer. It's soon April. We have been travelling for 45 days and there isn't long to go. After Torneträsk, the mountains disappear behind us and we are on flatter ground. Easy to make progress, no effort. We ski longer daily distances and take coffee breaks when the hot spring sun starts to burn our noses.

Then we reach the cement monolith that marks the triple meeting point between Sweden, Norway and Finland. Finally arrived. We take pictures of each other by the yellow block and celebrate with one energy biscuit each. Then we ski on. Time to go home.

In Finland we jump on a bus that takes us back to Sweden. Suddenly we cover 500 kilometres in just a few hours, and the speed feels almost unreal, as if we were flying.

The perspectives change if you go on a trek for 60 days.

THE GROUND IS BARE when I get back to my tent on 17 April, but otherwise everything is as I left it. I hang up my equipment, put away my sledge, spread out my reindeer hides and lie down on the bed. I see the sunlight pouring in through tiny holes in the canvas. I ought to get a new one. It is really worn.

I have seen huge swathes of Sweden and been skiing alongside a close mate of mine. We've got memories for life, but still I feel that long trips aren't my thing. I want to be in one place and start out from there. I want to run with light running shoes on my feet instead of stiff boots, want to feel the shocks right through my body.

The running shoes are hanging on the line. I get them down. At last a proper run for the first time in two months.

I set out without knowing how far or where I'll be going.

IN THE LATE SPRING, I run down to the college to see myself on TV. Peter's documentary about me is going to be broadcast on SVT. It's called *The Runner* and the indie band bob hund have done the music.

I see myself shivering in the Slagsån and running intervals across the coffee fields in Tanzania. Every image evokes memories that I can feel in my body: the way the air smells after an autumn shower or the crunching of the snow when it's seriously cold.

I am watching my life through Peter's eyes, and I see what he thinks is important. I listen to myself debating about stuff that is still buzzing around in my brain. *What is important? Which road should I take?*

The film ends with me saying: 'If I have to keep exposing myself to ever greater challenges in order to achieve the same emotions, then I must be doing something wrong.'

That's the part I like best in the whole film.

IN THE SUMMER, I TRAVEL south to Öckerö to work for a few weeks. I need money, and I need to swim to regain my suppleness after the winter and to exercise my feet and my fingers.

I work as a carer for Mum, and when she's too tired I settle her down on the sofa and cycle down to Hummerviken, where I can run across the rocks and dive in. The water is warm and everything feels effortless. I swim underwater, check out the brown seaweed and the tiny fishes that hide down there. I come back home after the swim with salt in my hair and tackle my assorted tasks: laundry, washing up, hoovering and shopping. Everything that makes Mum's everyday existence possible.

I think it's incredibly boring, but I do it because I must. I feel there's some kind of resistance like a bad memory in my body, which doesn't want to let go.

I'm cross with myself and with my spoilt attitude. I am wrong and I'm quite aware of that.

ONE MORNING I CARRY MUM up the highest rock on Öckerö. I make my way across boulders and heather, carrying her floppy body on my back. When we reach the top, we are met by a warm westerly wind that blows right into our faces. I settle Mum down on a large flat stone, with my arm round her waist so that she doesn't fall over.

We look out across the sea with Hyppeln, Rörö and Knippla to the north and Hönö and Fotö to the south. This is where I'm from, everything is familiar: the boats, the sea birds, and the warm, gentle air that smells of salt.

I want to be here, but at the same time I don't really.

I get an idea.

'Mum, do you want to come up to Jämtland with me?'

She thinks it sounds amazing. Dad is a bit doubtful and Grandma protests: 'Whatever will you do there?'

Grandad thinks we should go.

MUM is sleeping next to me in her special black seat, her head flopping to one side. My mate Johan is sitting in the back seat. He is also curious to see how I live up there.

We are on our way up to Jämtland in Mum's red Renault Kangoo. Every time I slow down, I have to put out my right arm and catch Mum so that she doesn't hit her face against the windscreen. She has no control over her body any more and weighs so little that the seat belt is activated only when I make an emergency stop.

In Sveg we take a break in the parking lot outside a store. I get some coffee and crumbly cookies, which I bring back to the car. Mum stays in her seat, drinking through a straw. The coffee goes down the wrong way and she can't get any breath and I have to bend her forward and slap her back. Outside, Johan is smoking his filterless roll-ups. When he started smoking long ago, he said that he was doing it to show everyone how easy it is to give up.

'How's the smoking working out?' I say. 'Weren't you meant to be giving up?'

He gives me the finger.

'It's bloody stupid to smoke,' I say. 'What do you think, Mum?'

'Absolutely,' she says.

After a long day's drive, we get to Undersåker and check in at the hotel Fjällsätra. Mum looks all contorted after sitting down the whole day. Johan and I carry her in together.

We have supper by the big windows with a view over the Indalsälven. Mum is too tired to talk, and I have to lean the wheelchair backwards so she doesn't fall face forward into her food. Afterwards we go into the toilet. It's not adjusted for wheelchair-users, and Johan has to hold on to Mum while I change her nappy.

'Mum, do you remember when Dad fell over and he got water up his bum when he was waterskiing? He looked so funny, what a face!'

Mum's face crumples until the tears start pouring out. I can't tell whether she's laughing or crying.

141

In our room I put her down on her stomach in the bed and she falls asleep at once. I change into my tracksuit and tie up my running shoes. On the other side of the bridge across the Indalsälven, I up the pace successively until I am running at full tilt on the road going up to Edsåsdalen. I follow this road until it ends and then turn round.

Thoughts are whirring in my head. I wonder how long Mum has got left. She is tough, of course. She is 46 and has been in a wheelchair for the last 16 years. Her muscles have gone and there's only soft skin left, but still she hasn't got a single grey hair on her head.

When I'm back at the hotel, I've run 20 kilometres in 70 minutes. I shower and crawl into bed next to Mum.

WE PARK UP BY HELGESJÖN. I crouch down next to the car and Johan helps me get Mum onto my back. Because she has no control, I have to walk bent forward so that her head doesn't loll back. It's like carrying a newborn baby.

We walk along the path that I have taken hundreds of times. Helgesjön is like a mirror and on the other side rises Åreskutan. We get into the forest, ducking under branches. The sun is shining through the trees, no mosquitoes. We've got one kilometre left.

When we get to the tent, I open the flap and carry Mum inside. Johan helps me put her on the bed. She's tired and needs a rest. There's a faint smell of smoke and reindeer hides, and she falls asleep straight away.

I light a fire and make some tea. Johan tells me that he's going to apply to become a salvage diver.

'But you've got the world's worst eyesight,' I say. 'And you're colour-blind.'

'I know all those colour charts by heart, so that's no problem,' he says.

'And what about your glasses, then?'

'It's just something wrong with the refraction and they can fix that.'

Johan changes the subject: 'So, why do you actually live up here? Why don't you just go to Alaska?'

Typical of him. Everyone else thinks that I am going too far, but he's challenging me to go further still. If I run 250 kilometres one week, he asks why I didn't run 500. And he's serious. He really wants to understand my thinking.

That's why it's so liberating to be with him. I never need to defend myself.

Mum wakes up. She barely speaks, just looks around. I don't need to explain why I live here. She can see that I am well and perfectly happy. That's enough for her.

We go back to the car and drive down to Hållandsgården for lunch. Mum wants coffee and biscuits, but they are out of biscuits. Then she says very loudly: 'I WANT A BISCUIT RIGHT NOW!'

I don't understand where that voice is coming from. The other people in the restaurant are staring at us.

'Take it easy, Mum. I'll go and ask.'

'BUT I WANT IT NOW!'

'OK, but pipe down. Don't be so bloody loud.'

The biscuit arrives and calm is restored. It must be the illness that makes her more upfront. When she says something, she has no filter. Like a child.

AFTER DRIVING FOR 900 KILOMETRES without stopping, the exhaust breaks down just as we drop Johan off on Hisingen. The car now sounds like a greaser's car with the roar vibrating right through the seats. Mum looks happy as we set off. I give it extra gas after each red light because it sounds so great.

Back on Öckerö I drive past Grandma and Grandad's house. I roll down the windows and rev up the engine in neutral until the noise echoes between the houses. Grandma wonders what's going on and comes out onto the balcony. She says something, but the noise from the engine makes it impossible to hear a single word. Mum laughs until she wheezes.

It feels great to watch Grandma's face when I bring Mum back so full of life and happiness.

I drive away in first gear. Grandma is still on the balcony shaking her head.

One of the desert fathers said: 'Nothing is as good for a beginner as insults. Whoever is insulted and copes with it is like a tree that is watered every day.'

Grandma has clearly taken on the role as the giver of insults as far as I'm concerned. It feels good to pay her back.

I say goodbye to Öckerö and take the bus into Gothenburg. The evening is warm, the air still. In the packed street cafés, people are drinking beer. They look bloated and red. Why do people want to live in the city and pay through the nose for a warm prison without views and without wind. Why live like animals cooped up in a cowshed?

I catch the night train and get to Järpen the following day.

WITH AN IRON FILE I smooth away every chip on the blade of the axe, and then I take out my sharpener and work it until the axe is as sharp as a knife. I've bought a new blade for the saw as well, which I attach to the handle.

This year I'm going to build up a supply of firewood that will last a bit longer through winter. The two earlier ones have run out far too quickly.

I leave the tent and walk away from Helgesjön and far into the woods. I walk around like a dizzy chicken for a while before finding a perfect dry fir tree. It has a diameter of at least 40 centimetres at the base, and is too big to saw down. I start chopping away, my back bent from my hips, and can feel the effort in my stomach muscles with each swing of the axe. It's like pushing myself across the ice on the lake against the wind.

It takes a good while to get it down. When it's done, I've just got to carry on: I have to chop it up into two-metre lengths. Not until I get closer to the top is the tree slender enough for me to be able to tackle it with the saw. The hours pass. My lower arms are feeling numb from all the effort. Finally I can chop off all the branches and start to drag the wood back home. It feels nice to be using my legs for a change.

I get the heavy logs back to the tent with my back straight and my legs bent. The lighter ones I can carry on my shoulders. Seven times there and back. When I'm done, I celebrate with smoked mackerel that I bought in Järpen. I love the greasy, smoky taste in my mouth. Afterwards I start to chop up the fir into smaller pieces. The following day I have to find another one.

I RUN ON THE GRAVEL ROAD towards Åre, past the Helgesjö-vallen and the Björn. The road is hard and the ground frost is starting to settle in. It's -5°C, the air is clear, there's no snow, but the frost is making the day look a little lighter.

I take the path that goes above the Fröå mine and run up towards Åreskutan. I get to a layer of snow which gets thicker the higher up I go. There are big holes across the toes of my shoes, but the worn-out soles are still just about there. As long as I keep running, it doesn't matter that it's slippery. The faster I run, the easier it is to keep my balance.

When the sun starts going down, it gets colder at once. My hands are frozen. I stop and eat some nuts that I've brought in a paper bag and I have to break the ice on a brook to get some water to drink. I start running back towards home.

I wave my arms about to warm up my fingers. I'm not used to the sub-zero temperatures yet. When I get home, my arms are cold right through, and my fingers are so stiff that I find it hard to undo my laces. I should have brought a spare sweater.

I keep the fire going until everything that was cold has been warmed up. I eat crispbread and some brown cheese and drink a litre of water with some honey. I am warming up from the inside out.

It's my third winter in the forest. Perhaps my life here doesn't have to be exactly like this.

JUST A FEW KILOMETRES from the tent, I find a little red cottage on the other side of the road going up to Helgesjön from Undersåker. The cottage lies at the edge of the forest above a meadow that slopes down towards the road, and it has a view across the valley. It's a bit run-down but nice, and years ago it was painted red. I like the matt, dry surface. I find out who owns it and ask if it is for sale. If I can find 150,000 kronor [$17,300], the cottage with the surrounding land is mine.

I borrow the money from Dad and become a homeowner. It all happens very fast.

The cottage was built at the end of the 19th century and rests on six flat stones. You enter from the north side through a simple door constructed from rough wooden boards. Inside, the ceiling is low – the people who lived there must have been short, probably because they worked hard and had a poor diet. The sun shines through the timbers of the thick walls. The floor is not insulated. In one corner, there's a crooked chimney above a fireplace made from grey slate, which takes up a quarter of the 20 square metres of floor space.

The cottage has two properly paned windows, one to the south and the other to the east, and along the west wall there's an inbuilt bunk. It's a little short, but if I lie diagonally from corner to corner I can stretch out.

It's an old-fashioned place for summer pasture; a long time ago, the cows used to spend the summer grazing in the meadows below.

Fifty metres away from the cottage there's a broken-down barn. I'm planning to turn it into firewood. Futher into the forest there's a well with fresh water.

There's a ferret living under the floorboards, the walls are full of voles and in the attic lives a boreal owl that I call Uffe.

I gather up all my stuff and move in.

A COLD RAIN IS FALLING FROM THE SKY. I'm in the house making an evening fire when Jocke drops in.

'You've got to phone home, Markus. Your dad wants to talk to you.'

It feels as if a balloon of sadness is inflating in my chest. Now she's dead.

I quickly pull on my running shoes and rush off to the village through the darkness, thinking of Mum. At the Hållandsgården I borrow a phone and Dad answers.

'It's not Mum, but Grandad is sick. It's been so quick. He's got liver cancer and is going to die very soon. We've just been told. If you want to say goodbye, you must come home at once.'

Dad has already bought a ticket for me, and I take the night train that evening.

GRANDAD IS LYING IN HIS BED when I walk through the door. His face is yellow, but he smells the same as ever, of soap and cold water.

'How are things?' I say.

'Well, what the doctor told me wasn't so nice. But it is what it is.'

He wants us to sing 'Blott en Dag' ('Day by Day') and all of us cousins sing the hymn in our rough voices. Grandad looks at me with his blue eyes.

'So, Markus, what are you actually up to? Why are you living all alone up there in the wilderness like that?'

He looks tired lying there and the whites of his eyes have gone yellow.

'Now make sure you find yourself a woman,' he says, looking serious. 'You marry her and let her make decisions for you. That would be the best thing for you.'

He doesn't say anything else. We help him get out of bed and he goes into the kitchen where Grandma has made Bohuslän cheesecake. Grandad is helped into his chair.

The whole family is there. On the table there are two different kinds of jam: cloudberry and strawberry. Grandad chooses cloudberry and it's the first time I've seen him put anything but strawberry jam on his cheesecake.

Later that evening I go and lie down on Grandma and Grandad's balcony. I sleep better outside in the cold. I'm lying under the eaves as a shelter from the cold. I watch the low clouds blowing by.

THE CHURCH IS PACKED OUT for Grandad's funeral. My cousins and I carry the coffin. The congregation sings 'Blott en Dag'.

Mum is sitting in her wheelchair at the front of the central aisle next to Grandma.

It's a relief that Grandad died before Mum.

LATER THAT AUTUMN, I GO DOWN TO Gothenburg for a friend's wedding. I arrive in the morning the day before the wedding and walk around the city streets like a normal person. I try to blend in, but I smell of smoke and I walk much more slowly than anyone else. Why are they all walking so fast? Everyone seems to have somewhere to go.

I take the tram to Marklandsgatan and walk, carrying my rucksack, up to Änggårdsbergen. Once there I change into my running gear and hide my rucksack beside a big boulder in the woods. I run off along paths that I recognise. I don't meet another soul. I can hear the hum of traffic from the Särö road, see the big crane at Eriksberg far off on the other side of the river.

I run past the 1000-metre slope where I used to do interval training. Now, when I compare it to the hills in Jämtland it looks quite flat. I carry on down towards Toltorpsdalen in Mölndal and run the outer circuit past the Sahlgrenska hospital and into the Botanic Gardens. My legs feel light and easy as I run through the trees, now in their leafless autumnal state, and get back to the stone after 90 minutes. I walk to a public water fountain that I know is still working, at the top of a hill between two old houses. I rinse myself in the cold water and change, brush my teeth and go back to the tram stop.

When the number one tram rolls off towards the city centre, I jump up onto the coupling behind the carriage and grab the rail with both hands, feeling the cold wind on my face. I experience the speed in a different way when I stand on the open-air platform. At the vegetable market I jump off and go into the covered market past counters groaning with fruit and displays of fresh red meat. I have some *fakes* soup at the Greek stall, filling up my stomach with lentils and garlic. I skip the white bread that only forms a ball of dough in my gut and instead buy some halva from an Arab chap at the exit before going back out into the grey damp air.

I am going to doss down with an old friend who lives up on the hill behind Gotaplatsen, inside and on a mattress for the first time in more than three-and-a-half years. On the way there, I pass the place where Johan and I stripped off and hid our clothes before running naked through the town. There are no leaves on the bushes now and the police would have seen us straight away.

When the evening comes, my mate and I go down a few flights of steps in the house to say hi to a girl he knows. And there she sits, wearing a red woolly jumper. The girl that I want. She hits me like a punch in the stomach. I have been celibate for a number of years, but now I am starting to feel something stirring.

She's called Frida and is studying at the college of design and crafts. We chat for a while and I get her telephone number.

A couple of days later I am back with Mum and Dad on Öckerö. I'm going to take the train to Jämtland the next day, but I'm not feeling relaxed about the prospect. I must give her a call. I think that she may be the one that Grandad was talking about. Dad says that I can borrow the car.

We meet at her place, and it's right, there's no doubt about it, something happening deep in my heart. I think she feels the same. Before I leave, she says that I have to decide on the spot what I want: 'Either we will be in touch and meet now and then, or else I don't give a damn. You can't go up to Jämtland and mess about and not be in touch and think that I will be sitting here missing you. I know that kind, so what do you want?'

'I'll be calling you,' I say.

As I leave, I feel as if I have some little birds fluttering away in my chest.

MY PEE TURNS INTO ICE before it hits the snow. The cold feels like a frozen landslide down my body, slipping down my back and along my legs towards the ground. When it is this cold, the amount of clothes I wear seems to make no difference.

I ski towards Järpen with a rucksack on my back. I have no option; I can't just sit in the tent feeding the fire any more. I've only got a bit of porridge oats left and I have to restock.

I ski calmly and methodically so that I don't start sweating because I don't want to create any dampness that will turn into ice the moment I stop. The snow is rough and unyielding. I have a thermos of warm water in my rucksack and matches in my breast pocket. If my feet seize up, I must be able to make a fire. When the cold really settles in the toes or fingers, it doesn't take long before the frostbite gets a grip.

The fourth winter. There have been many close shaves, the soles of my feet as white as chalk, my toes bloodless and stiff. No feeling. Thawing them out really hurts. The pain is incredible, like hitting your thumb with a hammer.

I'm wearing two of everything: two woollen sweaters under my anorak, two pairs of long johns under my cotton trousers, two pairs of socks, two pairs of gloves, two woolly hats. I've even pulled on a couple of woolly socks outside my boots. Grandma knitted them from especially hard-wearing wool.

A very low temperature on dry land is different from one in water. In the water, it feels like a powerful hug that you can't get out of, a solid cold, a numbing that goes deep within. On land, it's more sneaky; it starts in the fingers and the feet and works its way slowly further and further into the body.

When I arrive in Järpen, I go to the cashpoint to make a withdrawal. I have 1600 kronor [$185]. Good, that's enough to keep me going for two months. I go into the supermarket and buy what I need: lentils, grains, dried fruit, butter, frozen peas, apples and a lollipop that I pop in my mouth at once.

I strap on my skis and set off for home. The snow holds the skis well and I don't need to wax them. When the rucksack is full, it pinches my shoulders and stops the blood flow to the arms. Every 20 minutes, I have to stop and quickly swing my arms backwards 50 times, pushing the warm blood from my heart back out into my fingers.

When I get back to the house, my face is frozen and I'm tired and hungry. I light up the range with my stiff fingers and replace the hard, cold skiing boots with soft, warm woollen slippers. I eat a soup made from lentils, salt, thyme and frozen peas. I grill an apple for afters.

ONE FRIDAY, SHE ARRIVES ON THE TRAIN AT UNDER-SÅKER. I cycle there on a borrowed bike, a mountain bike with wide tyres. The road is slippery, but if I cycle fast I'm all right. I'm waiting on the platform when the train comes screeching into the station.

When Frida gets off the train, she's wearing a worn-out old anorak and is carrying a small rucksack. This minimalist packing tells me a lot.

I'm not seized with panic when I see her. I don't want to run away.

She has to sit on the handlebars as I cycle back home, and I carry her rucksack on my back. There's a light headwind blowing as I struggle up the long uphill stretches. Her hair is tickling my face – the strands of her hair are thinner than Mum's. They are itchier. I assume that her bum must be hurting on the hard handlebars, but she doesn't mention it.

When we arrive at the cottage, some snow has blown and settled on the floor just inside the door. It's been like that for a while, the heat just doesn't seem to reach that spot. I make a fire in the range and light a few candles. I start cooking, frying some minced beef and frozen cabbage and add a little oil and salt.

'So this is where you live, Markus?' she says.

'Yes, this is where I live.'

Frida sits at the table and looks out, still wearing her hat and thick woollen sweater. It feels as if she can look right through me. The temperature begins to rise in the cottage from below to above zero.

'How do you spend your days, then?'

'I get up, I eat, I run, I try not to freeze. I do what I like. I want to have a lot of time to do not very much.'

'But how do you manage to put food on the table?'

'It's as easy as anything. When I have less than 400 kronor [$45] in my account, I get some kind of job that will pay me a bit of money.'

We spend the whole day inside the house, putting log after log on the fire. In the evening, Frida borrows my winter sleeping bag. She can sleep in the top bunk where it's warmest.

When we wake up the next day, the temperature in the cottage is below zero again. Frida looks frozen and hungry. I make some porridge, heat the water on my camping stove and light the range. We huddle up close in front of the fire with a blanket wrapped around us We eat the porridge with grated carrots instead of jam.

I am starting to think about children, I feel a bit broody. I think about naked skin.

As the heat returns to the cottage, our sentences become ever longer. The sun shines in through the thin, cracked window pane.

Frida sits down at the table. She has got some college work that she has to finish. I can see that she's good at what she's doing. She draws effortlessly. I go for a run.

On Sunday evening I cycle back to the train station with her on the handlebars. It's colder and not quite as slippery. No wind.

The train arrives and she gets on it. I think that she's going to get herself a cup of coffee. I don't drink coffee, but when she comes next I'll buy a packet.

WHEN SPRING COMES, we move in together in a little stone cottage on Öckerö. It feels weird to sleep indoors with a thick roof over my head and another person next to me. I'm lying on a soft mattress, I don't hear any birds, just her quiet breathing.

I'm back on the island for the first time in nearly five years. I've no idea how this will work out and that's OK.

Frida is steady and really straightforward. When I look at her, I don't long for anything else.

MUM IS LYING ON THE SOFA. The sun is shining on her face and she looks tired. Her legs are like dead wood. There is no longer any connection between her brain and her feet.

Mum is happy to have met Frida. I can see that in her eyes. Frida has got a cold and is sitting at the table swotting for an exam. Mum wants to sit up, and Frida eases her legs onto the floor and pulls her up into a sitting position.

'Sickness. Leave, Frida, now,' says Mum.

ONE LATE SUMMER'S DAY, Mum comes home from a stay at a hospice in Skåne down in the south of Sweden. Suddenly there she is, three days early. 'She just wanted to go home,' says the carer.

I go across to Mum in the evening. She's lying on her front in the bed, sleeping, her head to one side. The blind is rolled down. She is wearing a white nightie.

I lie down next to her. She doesn't wake up, she must be tired after the journey. She smells the same as always.

'See you tomorrow,' I say.

I close the door behind me and go out through the garage.

The next morning, I'm woken up by my younger sister Ida. She's standing in the door with tears running down her cheek and says that Mum is dead.

'She died in the night, Markus. The nurse phoned us.'

We go over there in Ida's car. Mum is lying there all pale in her bed. Whatever was her has gone.

There would never be any healing.

My siblings, Dad and I stand there in the room with Mum in the bed. Someone has turned her onto her back. I don't understand anything, I was just here 10 hours ago.

We walk down to Saltars and out across the rocks, my siblings and I. We have brought fruit and water. The sun is shining from a clear blue sky. It is the most beautiful day of the summer. The air temperature is 27°C, the water 22°C. The sea lies still, shining like a mirror. For the last stretch my younger brother runs off in long strides like an elk, and my sisters and I follow. We fly through the air, competing for who can leap the furthest. My brother wins by one whole metre.

Mum would have been happy if she had been with us, she would have sat laughing on the rock. I feel a mixture of heaviness and relief.

I swim underwater in my own tears.

TEN YEARS LATER

I'M RUNNING IN THE DARKNESS across the ice on Helgesjön. The evening is cold and full of stars, the moon is just a thin crescent. The ice is shiny and free of snow, it's like running on a dark mirror. I feel the ice tensing and creaking beneath my feet. It's making hollow sounds.

I run towards a warm, orange light from a lone 60-watt bulb in one of the farms on the other side of the lake. All alone in the world.

I'm wearing tights and double sweaters and an anorak. I've pulled on a pair of thick woolly mittens that cover my forearms up to my elbow. My hands and feet are warm. There's ice in my beard. A perfect mixture of warmth and cold.

On the other side of the lake I follow the gravel road down to Undersåker. Before I cross over the E14, I walk through the farm where the Boxer and I stayed for a sports camp two years before he died. That was 20 years ago.

Shit, I'm almost 40. When Dad was that age, I thought that he was really old.

I leave the lamps of Undersåker behind and go back into the darkness on the other side of the Indalsälven. I like it when the light disappears and I can run like a shadow in the grey dusk. I don't meet anyone. I get the same feeling as always: without this, my life would be poorer.

I think that every run may be my last, and so I savour it.

I pass Hålland on the way home, passing Hållandsgården and the brown brick walls of the college. Places that have helped me to become who I was meant to be. After an hour and 50 minutes I'm back home, my body still feeling light. The old red cottage is gone, but the place still looks the same.

The old house was too far gone; I think that at least 500 hundred voles were living under the floor. I burned the whole place down one day 10 years ago when summer was at its warmest and the grass at its tallest. It was quite a blaze. The nearest trees were singed and it was a bit worrying when the flames were at their highest and I was standing by with just one small bucket of water, but the forest survived.

I just drew a simple sketch of Frida's and my new house and made a quick calculation of the materials we would need. Using 200,000 kronor [$23,000] out of the money I inherited from Mum, I ordered a load of planks from a sawmill beyond Järpen. I skipped the building permit; I couldn't be bothered with the bureaucracy, I just got going. A labourer from the area helped me cast the concrete plinths and then Mats from Backen's timber yard came over with the planks on his old truck. We unloaded everything by hand; it took a whole day.

As I looked at the planks, I felt a surge of adrenaline. It was up to me to put up this house before the wood rotted. That was the simple truth of the matter.

I'd never built a house before, but I do like woodwork.

The first few weeks I had no power, so I sawed up all the supporting beams and the studs by hand. My upper arms got incredibly strong. Eventually I bought a diesel-powered generator and borrowed an electric saw and sawed up the panelling planks and the plywood boards. I insulated the whole house with cellulose foam – 35 centimetres thick in walls and 45 centimetres in the roof – so that I wouldn't have to burn so much wood in the winter.

I worked 16 hours a day. I felt no tiredness, no hunger. There was a constant injection of energy in my body.

The price I had to pay came later on when the house was finished and the adrenaline had stopped pumping. Then I was exhausted for several months.

Frida is sitting on the sofa feeding the baby when I come in. Both fireplaces are going and the ice in my beard is melting and dripping onto the floor.

Birgitta is one week old and named after Mum. We have not given her a bath yet, and she still smells of amniotic fluid and blood. I feel her pulse beating quick and light when I hold my warm hand against her head.

Our other girls, Signe and Helga, are sleeping up in the attic.

ONE DAY, FRIDA ASKS ME why I always run twice a day.

'You walk around aching and investing a lot of energy in your training, energy that could be used for the family.'

'But I like running,' I say.

'I know, but is it so much less fun to go running just once a day? Will your body feel different then? Will you run more slowly? Anyway, that isn't the reason that you run.'

She says it calmly, looking at me with her light blue eyes. I can see that she has been thinking this for a while. There's no irritation in her voice, just a calm question straight from her heart.

We are sitting at the table, drinking red tea. I have no sensible answer for her. This is just something that I've done for so long: got up in the morning and run, and done the same thing in the evening, every day for 20 years. It's a habit that is so firmly entrenched in my body and I have no intention of changing.

Frida earns most of the money for the family when she is not on maternity leave. She works with stuff she's really good at; she chooses the colours for Volvo cars. It's extraordinary that she can master so many different things. I'm amazed that love can grow year after year. It's different now from when we met, the roots are deeper.

At the same time, I think that it can all go pear-shaped, I take nothing for granted. That's why I think it works.

As for myself, I support the family whenever I get the chance: I get work on building sites, or as a carer, or with boys who have got into trouble with the law and have ended up in a local institution. Peter's film, *The Runner*, also made me into a source of inspiration for some of Sweden's aspiring runners, and due to the growing fitness bug I am increasingly called on to deliver lectures or work as a trainer.

Sometimes I think that the present interest in running can't be sustained and that the bubble will burst, that it will all run out and be absorbed by the earth. For me, it doesn't make any difference. I will continue using my legs to make new discoveries.

I WALK PAST THE STOCKHOLM stadium, leaving the cars, the traffic lights and the smelly exhausts behind and carry on out to Fiskartorpet, an area for outdoor activities located within the elegant rustic urban environment of Djurgården. I've brought my rucksack with a sleeping bag and a sleeping mat, and at the bottom of the bag are my running shoes and training gear.

I'm giving a talk at the Grand Hôtel and I turned down the offer of a room the night before. It's nice to sleep in soft beds, but the rooms are always so hot. I sleep better outside and have to grab my opportunities when I'm away from my family. Also it brings back memories and feelings that I can use when I give my lecture. Sleeping in the open air is like a warm-up.

A little bit away from the lodge at Fiskartorpet I find a flat piece of ground by a copse near the water. I clear away some twigs and branches, roll out the mat and take out the sleeping bag. I peel off the top layer of clothes and crawl into the sleeping bag.

The sky is clear and it's 10°C. I'm lying on my back looking up at the sky; my body is warm and my face is cool. The light from the city is leaking out so that the starlight can't quite break through. I hear the traffic noise from afar.

When I wake up the next morning, there is a thin sheen of dew over the sleeping bag. I put on my training gear and set off. I run through the Lill-Jansskogen, past bare trees with their intricate patterns of naked branches, and carry on towards the city centre. I am running calmly through the streets, side by side with pedestrians, cyclists and cars. I follow Söder Mälarstrand to the bridge leading to Långholmen, I pass the wharf and run below the Västerbron. I do two quick circuits around Långholmen, which warms up my body and then run all the way back to Fiskartorpet.

The morning sun shines weakly through the branches and the dew is still on my sleeping bag when I get back. I take all my stuff down to the water, where I strip naked and jump in. The water is brackish, a mix between the west coast and Helgesjön. Ice cold.

I arrive at the Grand Hôtel 30 minutes before I'm due to speak and walk into the energy-rich heat. My head is ready, nervous but charged. I feel a tremendous pressure in my head, of words that want to get out.

In the audience, there are 500 people in long, silent rows. They are here to celebrate the Oscars of the Swedish food industry, the contest called Arlatävlingen Golden Cow. Some people on the floor are nominated for prizes like Environmentalist of the Year, Altruistic Food Producer of the Year, Most Cheerful Food Shop of the Year, Cook of the Year, and they are all waiting nervously to discover the winners. But first I will speak for exactly 50 minutes. There is a clock on the stage, which I am told to keep an eye on.

I know roughly how I will begin, and after that nothing's planned. Just the way I want it.

I hear the moderator introducing me over the loud speakers. Fifteen seconds to go. I walk up the steps and on stage. It feels a bit unreal to stand in front of all these people who are waiting for me to say something. But I don't feel any panic. The contact is there, a vent opens into the brain, and thoughts formed during silent months come out. I talk of darkness, cold and hunger and how life in the forest helped me discover what I wanted to do.

I am surprised every time that it works out. That I, who used only to feel at home in the physical world, can stand up in front of people without losing it. The fact is that I actively enjoy doing this.

At school I was always given low marks for oral presentation. But I was never asked to talk about anything that I liked.

That's what it is all about: finding your thing. That's when it happens.

ONE DAY WHEN I AM WALKING with my older girls, we pass the place where I parked Mum's car when she had come to see me. I take Signe and Helga to the path where I carried Mum on my back many years ago. It's almost overgrown now, and doesn't show any trace of when I walked along it, ducking under all those trees.

The decision to leave the tent happened so quickly, like a sunrise in Tanzania. I took the most important stuff with me – the axe, the canvas cover and the thick sleeping bag – and just left the rest.

Ten years later and the frame of the tent is still there. The bed is still resting on the stones, with my light green synthetic sleeping bag wet and torn on top. The reindeer skins are gone, probably eaten by hungry animals and birds. The box with spices and lentils is lying beneath a tree nearby.

It all feels recent but also very long ago that I lived here for those four years. What I miss most of all is the feeling when I crept into the sleeping bag in the evening and could see the stars through the smoke hole and my breath rose from my mouth like a damp cloud. I was enveloped by the darkness and cold as I slept, and woke up warm, strong and hungry after 11 hours of dreamless sleep.

'Why did you live here, Dad?' asks Signe.

'Because I wanted to,' I say.

That's enough, there are no further questions. To children, everything is normal; they're not judgemental and nothing is too strange. They take in what they want to take in.

I AM BOUNCING VIOLENTLY OVER THE bumps on the road up to Vålådalen. I really should change the car's rear shock absorbers, but I like driving around in a run-down car that you don't have to be too careful with. I change the oil and the filter and look after the engine, and I don't give a damn about the rest.

It's late summer, no snow even on the mountain peaks, only greenery, firs and mountain birch. I am driving with the windows down and I feel the warm wind. The windscreen is covered in dead mosquitoes. Dad would not have been impressed if he'd seen it.

The Swedish cross-country skiers are attending a camp in Gunder Hägg's old stomping ground. I'm going to teach running technique to the skiers on Vålådalen's cinder track, working on the positioning of the feet and hips to lessen the risk of damage during their long, snow-free season. Running is a perfect tool for locating the body's weaknesses, like a natural screening process where every planting of the foot is transmitted through the body and makes it react at the point of weakness.

All skiers are outstandingly fit, but many of them run in a sitting position and so can be afflicted with runners' knees and painful Achilles tendons. I understand how easily this can happen: they look at running as a way of building up their fitness and don't take into account that their technique is just as important there as when they are skiing. If you listen to them, they talk a lot about their capacity to absorb oxygen and the importance of having a strong engine, but if the power is not directed correctly they won't get the maximum out of the energy they expend. It's like money – it doesn't matter how large your salary is if you fritter away everything that you earn.

It's fun to work with people who are passionate about what they do and are alone within their bodies for many hours of every day. They are shaped by the hours of training in the forest or on the mountain, and in that I completely understand them.

I begin with the women and carry on with the men. They run diagonals across the football pitch while I observe their steps.

Many of them move well right from the start. They run upright with their hips pushed forward so that their feet land straight below their body, giving them a natural forward movement. They are flowing. Others move in completely the wrong way, running with a bent-over trunk and their bottom sticking out so that the body is shaped like an S. Their feet hit the ground a bit in front of their body, the power goes down through their heels and they have to make that much more of an effort. They are always braking as they advance.

I tell the skiers to take off their shoes, and at once they all run better. I often give this advice and the same thing happens every time: when the foot makes direct contact with the ground, the foot itself can feel how it wants to land.

I can't understand why there are so many rubbish shoes about with thick soles making it hard to run in the way that we are designed to do. Running is simple, and that is its strength. Everyone can run. It doesn't cost anything. You don't need shoes developed by NASA.

But it can be easy to forget this when there's a whole industry turning out new products and all the time delivering new answers to problems that were solved long ago.

I MYSELF TRIED TO RUN ALONG THE SWEDISH mountain range a few years ago, 1300 kilometres across rough terrain where Stig-Mikael and I once went on our skiing adventure. Nobody had done it before and I wanted to see if it was possible.

I ran with a map, compass, a GPS, some spare clothes and food for the day in my runners' rucksack. I didn't need to bring any more stuff because I had a sponsor who had organised a support car, which carried more equipment and food to places that I would pass along the road. The plan was to run 50–60 kilometres a day for nearly a month.

I ran in my ordinary clothes and shoes, but on my feet I wore something that I had never used before: a pair of compression socks. They are firm across the ankles and the pressure up the legs diminishes gradually and makes the blood pump more easily through the veins. Compression stockings have been used in the healthcare system for ages, by people who don't move enough after an operation or because they are old. They stop blood clots and embolisms, and are also used by people on long flights. A few years ago they began to be advertised for use by sportspeople. It is said that recuperation happens faster when there's pressure around the foot and calf, and I thought that there would be no harm in trying it out.

I started off in Kilpisjärvi at the end of July and ran over the mountains to the Three Countries monument, ran along rocky paths with the summer sun shining from a blue sky. Life was simple. I slept and bought food in the huts run by the Swedish Tourist Association, and ran on my own between the round, gentle slopes. I drank cold mountain water. In Rostojauri I filled my rucksack with sausage and chocolate wafers, and the following three days I ran 60–90 kilometres a day, across shallow streams and dank marshes with low willow trees, the reindeer my only company. I was where I wanted to be, left to myself and my own decisions.

When I had passed Abisko and run on southwards on Kungsleden, my feet began to swell up and I got terrible blisters on my toes. When I took off my shoes, my feet were four sizes bigger than normal. I couldn't recognise them.

Had my kidneys broken down and was that why there was so much fluid in my feet? In a mountain hut, I cut away the front of my shoes to make room for my feet. I carried on southwards with spongey feet and pain in the tendons coming from the toes.

I started to sleep with the pillow under my feet to see if a long sleep during the night would get rid of the fluid. No improvement. If I pressed my thumb into the top of my foot, it left a hollow which didn't go away for a long while, like a thumb mark in warm butter.

After 380 kilometres in one week, I arrived at Saltoloukta. My feet were swollen like those of an old man with heart problems. I decided to take a day of complete rest and see if the swelling went down. No bloody difference.

I looked at my black support stockings. Could they be the cause?

The next day, I ran on in woollen socks and sandals instead. The swelling disappeared at once.

Those damn stockings – how could I have fallen for that hard sell? I was incredibly annoyed with myself for not having thought logically: how smart is it to have something tight around your legs for 10 hours every day?

This is something that I find really disturbing: all the useless stuff being developed, which in many cases is just about consumption.

I carried on running for another 380 kilometres. The swelling didn't come back, but the pain was still there: the fluid in my feet had made me put my weight through my legs in an unnatural way, and my body didn't manage to recuperate. The area around the tendons became inflamed and half my little toe seemed to be gone, lost because of the world's biggest blister. Every step seemed to cut directly into the soles of my feet; it was the same feeling as in Austria when my instep collapsed.

166

Less than 500 kilometres from the end I had to make a decision: give up or force myself on just to have done it. To have accomplished it. So that nobody could say that I had failed. It would be totally possible to walk the last section down to Grövelsjön.

But if I did, I would be back in that destructive pit which I recognise so well, the pit where I don't listen, into which no light can reach and where the walls are slippery.

I went back to my family instead. When I got there, they were out swimming. I jumped in and swam with Signe on my back.

For me, it was not a failure. It was one of the best things I've ever done.

WE ACQUIRE A FEW SUMMER SHEEP that graze in the meadow beside the house. Five rams that walk around like lawnmowers and grow bigger and stronger every day.

From a local egg producer, we buy five retired hens for 35 kronor [$4] each. After 54 weeks in the egg factory, they are naked and frozen and have barely any feathers on their bodies, like ready-prepared chickens in the freezer, only with legs and heads and beating hearts.

I build a little chicken coop at the edge of the forest. We give them our leftovers – cold porridge, peelings from potatoes and vegetables, and scraps of meat and fish and for this they pay us with eggs. After just a few weeks, they start to grow and get splendid white feathers. The egg yolks become ever more yellow and their cones become redder for every day that they can eat and live their lives at their own pace. They are transformed into the hens in Pettson and Findus [a popular series of children's books]. They are – unofficially – the world's most amazing birds. They are incredibly funny to watch as they run around on their scrawny legs. Every time I feed them, they act as if they've won the lottery – they cackle and flap their wings and their life is as good as it gets. Everyone who can should get themselves some chickens.

Every morning Helga and Signe go out to collect the eggs. They come back proud and happy and longing for pancakes. Frida makes a thick mixture of spelt flour, milk and our own eggs. Then I fry the pancakes in lots of butter.

Frida and the children tuck in, because it tastes good and they are hungry, and nowadays I eat like them. Without anxiety, without judgements or all sorts of ideas.

What a lot of food fads I have tried over the years: no carbohydrates, only carbohydrates, vegan food, a protein diet. Nothing worked because my head wasn't engaged.

What started as an idea that vegetables were good for you ended with me eating nothing but vegetables, and if I didn't stick to this I was seized by a feeling of panic. Food just meant feelings; I didn't concern myself with my body or with hunger.

When I look back on my teenage years, it's obvious that I ate far too little. Long days with double training sessions, and muesli and fizzy drinks when I got home in the evening. Nobody kept an eye on what I was eating: my trainer didn't care, Mum lay exhausted in her bed, and Dad had other things to worry about. For myself, I didn't understand how everything was connected. I had become slow and stupid because there was too little energy in my blood. No wonder school didn't work out.

Tanzania was the same: I got this fixed idea in my head and it grew into something that I could not resist. It didn't seem to matter that in my body it all felt wrong.

Everything depends on what goes on inside your head. It sounds self-evident, but for me this has been tricky.

The world of sports training is full of advice on food, nutrition and ready-made diets, but my own experiences have made me cautious. I don't think that you can hide behind a diet or a theory. It's like avoiding any blame and placing responsibility with someone else. You can't expect any blessings to be simply doled out.

Only you yourself can come to realise what it is that makes you feel good. If you accept full responsibility and your head is at peace as you eat, your body will absorb what it needs.

But it is hard to package and market a product called 'Your own responsibility'. There's no money to be made that way, and that is the reason why there are so many different diets.

At the kitchen table Signe is tucking in with huge bites and Helga with small ones. The two of them have come from Frida and myself, but they could just as well have come from different continents. Signe is blonde, Helga is dark. One loves proper food and one prefers sugar, like me. One loves to be hugged and the other doesn't and prefers to wrestle. One is tired at night and the other in the morning.

I stand in the window and follow them with my eyes as they walk down our hill to the road. Their slender legs and arms are tanned after the summer; they are wearing sandals, shorts and vests. Each is wearing a backpack, with some fruit in the outside pocket. They are waiting for the communal taxi that will take them to their school in Undersåker. They are expectant and happy. Full of energy.

It took time for me to become a dad, before I let go of my big ego and opened the door into my heart. Before I saw the girls.

To be a dad requires the same thing as living out there in the cold: presence.

I RUN ACROSS ONE OF THE MARSHES on the slopes beyond the forest behind our house. It's like running in soft butter; I sink down to my midriff in the deepest hollows. Gentle on the calves. I am wearing only shoes and a pair of running shorts and feel the warm evening sun against my back.

When I arrive at our little beach at Helgesjön, Signe and Helga run naked along the water, their bottoms as brown as the rest of their bodies. I am happy the longer they remain unselfconscious about their bodies. The longer they just are. Birgitta and Frida are lying on a blanket under a sunshade.

I jump in the water and Helga climbs up on my back. With her hanging there, I swim out with Signe to the swimming platform. The water is 24°C. It's been a great summer in Jämtland, the sun has shone from a blue sky every day.

I know that this is a memory that I will carry with me for the rest of my life.

It will stay in my body as something wonderful, and it will still be there when I am old.

FRIDA IS SITTING ON THE FLOOR, painting, oil on canvas. A dark horizon beyond the sea or mountains.

Total concentration, it looks amazing. The world outside doesn't exist. The children are asleep and it is her moment. She does it for herself. It is something that has to be expressed and does not have to be shown to other people.

I run and she paints – the same focus but on different things.

SOMETIMES I GET VISITORS to our place in the mountain pastures. They come from all around the world and spend a few days in a guest house that I built a little bit away from our own.

Together we live the simple life – making fires, preparing food outside and washing ourselves in the sauna after several hours of running. Living the life that helped me to make my head connect with my body – a life that can benefit everyone. A few days without stress, where running becomes a way of opening up your heart.

Of course, those who come here are keen to know about training and a lot of practical things, but sooner or later I'm also asked the same questions that I used to ask myself, questions that are still with me, *What is it that makes us feel well? What is it that makes life worth living?*

I know how tempting it is to come up with an answer. It would be so simple to be black and white, to point emphatically and send people off in one direction. To heaven or hell.

But I don't know how others should live their lives. I know only that the forest and running happened to help me to find my way. So I can talk only about myself and then answer with another question. *What do you yourself feel, what do you think your way looks like?*

For many, running becomes a matter of consumption, a matter that has to be accounted for and be superseded. Just another achievement in a life that is all about achieving things on every level. I believe that that sort of thinking is mistaken. Freedom in movement disappears if it is reduced to something comparative. It becomes bureaucracy, running in ordered rows along a fixed, predetermined path.

Running is the movement of a free human being. It doesn't demand any special premises or machines. You only need to put on your shoes and get going. Let the blood circulate. Then everything becomes much clearer.

A FEW YEARS AGO, I RAN the big race around Gothenburg. When I collected my number the day before the race, the athletics building was jam-packed with people. The atmosphere was great, there was so much energy in the air – the way there always is when tens of thousands of people with the same goal are gathered together in the same place.

Some people came up to me and asked if I was the fellow in the documentary *The Runner*. It felt a bit weird but nice. The film stands for something that I like.

The sports hall was full of entrepreneurs who were seizing the opportunity to sell their products: long tights, short tights, spring clothes, summer clothes, winter clothes and autumn clothes; black clothes, white clothes and clothes in colourful synthetic material that is visible from far off; shoes that breathe and shoes that don't, shoes with and without shock absorbers, shoes with ice-spikes, 'barefoot shoes', and 'African Masai shoes'; watches with inbuilt GPS and altitude gauges, watches with pulse monitors, watches that can be connected to your computer so that your run can be automatically registered and entered on a digital chart. Everything produced with the help of the very latest super-duper technology.

So much stuff in order to practise something that is so simple.

Around the tables was a crowd of runners waiting for the next day's start. Who were being geed up by the mass of people, and who wanted to experience running alongside other people. Who used this race as their motivation to train for the rest of the year.

I understood the festive atmosphere and the joy, while at the same time I felt that what I am about is something quite different. There and then, it became so clear to me. Running is something that I want to do on my own, in worn-out clothes. I don't want to run with other people, as part of a procession.

I run because I want to. Not in order to achieve. I've already been there and I'm beyond that.

I meet so many people who want to run fast. It is their only goal, the one that counts. And then they get panicky when they don't measure up – because there is always something to improve, seconds to be shaved off. I know what it's like.

My salvation was when I skipped all that stuff and removed everything that could be measured: distances, speeds and times. Things that inspire some people but hold back many more.

I think that the challenge of our time is to just call a halt to all that.

Whose thoughts are in my head if I never have time to think? If I never look at my life from outside, if it's never silent?

Not mine anyway.

THE NEXT DAY I STOOD behind the tape in the first group of runners. Lots of people in Slottsskogen, and the smell of grilled sausages in the air. Relaxed African runners next to me, which reminded me of my friends in Tanzania, Mama Gwandu's chicken, the lightning over Kilimanjaro. Another life, another time.

We were off.

I disappeared into myself, the outside world vanished. Instead I ran on my own, breathing deeply on a gravel road above Norsjön. I felt my heart. I saw the mountains shining in the late summer sun, and my back was naked and tanned.

Everything was clear: my head, the air, my thoughts.

SOME FINAL THOUGHTS

When I took the train northwards nearly 20 years ago, I had no inkling that I would write a book or do a lecture tour about my experiences and what I learned about living on my own in the woods for four years.

It was not a social experiment I was undertaking, it was a survival strategy. In that place, at that moment, it was the best thing for me to do. Without the forest I don't think that I would be alive today. The woods, the darkness and the cold helped me to find the way back to the real me. Those long winter months made me shed everything that was inessential. No TV, no adverts, no artifice. Only my thoughts and myself. I needed to be in that sort of enviroument to discover what I really wanted to do with my life.

I am not unique. I have no superpowers. But when I want something, I give it all I've got, 100 per cent – that is my strength. When I moved up there, I was just a young man with a lot of running in his legs and a heart full of anguish.

I have no truths to offer nor answers to give, just directions that I think we humans we would do well to follow. In the course of our lives, we will encounter opposition; that happens to all of us. It is part of what it means to be human. I ran into a lot of opposition myself when I was young, and the woods became my way of coping.

I will lay out here what I learned, insights that I still carry with me. Advice, if you like.

Motivation is one of the most important things that we humans possess. It is the engine for everything. It fills you with energy, so that you can do incredible things, things that look impossible from the outside.

I can understand that the life I lived in the forest may look weird from the outside. Why live like that when you could be inside in the warmth? This is where the motivation comes in. I wanted to live outside. I wanted to find something that I didn't have. I wanted to fill the emptiness that I felt within. I thought that I could find all that in the forest and I was motivated to test it out and expose myself to whatever the seasons would send my way.

The motivation persisted in the face of hunger and cold and thousands of mosquitoes.

It persisted so that I was on the right side of the borderline.

I had to accept responsibility, to listen to myself.

And take seriously whatever I might feel.

* * *

If you are never silent and never look at yourself from the outside, you will end up living a life that isn't yours.

To be still is a way of finding the hunger and the driving force to achieve something really meaningful, something that connects your head to your body. Something that brings a sense of calm and presence in the moment. That makes you sleep deeply.

That calm and that presence in the moment don't just happen. For me, it has been tough to achieve and I am still working on it.

That was my first battle in the woods. After a couple of weeks on my own, my body seemed to be twitching. I experienced an enormous restlessness and felt the need to find something to stimulate my brain.

But I thought that perhaps I could learn something if I conquered this restlessness.

Maybe there was something beyond this. Something that has nothing to do with achievement. That I am good enough as I am.

It took me a couple of months of sitting on a tree stump in the woods before the restlessness went.

That time was a good investment. Life became greater after that.

Food tasted better and the song of the birds in the woods was even lovelier.

Switch off your phone. Take a walk in the nearest woods without music in your ears, only in your head.

Go on your own, and be a little afraid of the dark.

Experience that feeling of restlessness. Stay in that feeling for a moment.

When you get back home, light a candle. You think different thoughts in front of a living flame than before a light bulb. Let that burning candle be your television for the night.

* * *

When I lived in the forest, the questions and problems were often simple to solve.

They tended to concern my basic needs – that I was hungry, tired or freezing.

I faced these problems every day and it was easy to find the solution.

To eat, sleep or light a fire. If I did that, all was well again.

In the times that we are living in now, the questions are more complex. More in the head, further away from our basic needs – and not as easy to solve.

That is why it is important to rest your head now and then and let your thoughts come and go without focusing too much on each one.

Are you facing an important decision and don't know what to do?

Put on your shoes, open up the door and start walking. Walk a long way and keep walking until the decision has taken shape.

In your blood there is nourishment and the solutions to problems, which is why it is important to let the blood circulate a little faster, to raise the pulse rate sometimes.

* * *

To place yourself sometimes in situations where all your needs are not met can raise your sensitivity.

We have arrived at a level in society where all our needs are constantly satisfied. If we really want to feel something, it must be of a very special quality. I think this is the first time in human history that we must actively learn how to shed some of what we have.

To do without.

To realise that more isn't always better.

Today we don't need to choose between good and evil, between having enough to eat or starving.

Now we choose between good and good. Paint the kitchen white or grey. Have fish or meat for dinner.

I don't think we feel more enjoyment or satisfaction by having a bigger or faster car, by having more delicious sweets or more food.

I think what we need is the opposite: to do without in order to raise our sensitivity.

To do without in order to feel more, to feel the taste of food after two days of fasting. To feel how wonderful it is to get into a hot bath when you have been out in the cold weather for a whole day.

* * *

There's no reason to worry about death. As I came about from nothing, it must be a simple matter for God to allow me to stay on in some other form after the end of my life.

My grandfather lived his whole life out at sea, on a wooden fishing boat alongside his brothers. He fished all the year round off the coasts of Iceland, Norway and Scotland. An open horizon in every direction. He knew that the sea was vast and sometimes merciless. He knew that he couldn't control the wind, the storms or the waves. And that was OK. Sometimes it very nearly ended badly.

The hull of the ship creaked in the waves and the engine struggled. Grandad accepted what he couldn't change.

That is what I learned for myself in the forest.

I can't control all the things around me. The only thing that I can control is my attitude to what is happening. That thought, combined with my chosen faith in a life after this one, gives me great peace of mind.

* * *

Now we have arrived at the last lines of this book.

Put on your shoes, open the door and go out on the streets and the paths. Run through the woods.

Run without a watch. See your heart. Let your blood circulate.

Think big thoughts.

The forest awaits.

Markus Torgeby, 2018

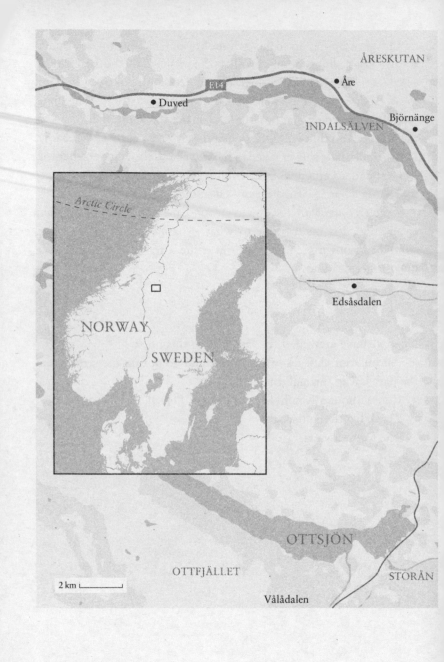

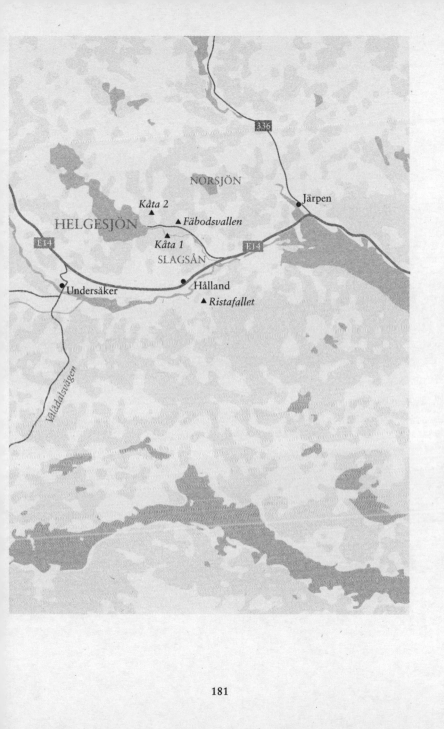

ACKNOWLEDGEMENTS

I want to thank my family for putting up with me although it can't always have been so easy: Elin, Ida, Gustav, Dad and Mum in heaven and my three daughters, thank you for giving me some perspective on life.

I also want to thank my childhood mates, Fredrik Lardmo, Peter Lindquist, Anders Palm, Mikael Simonsson and Johan Werubo, for always being there. And Mikael Kjellberg – thank you for introducing me to Frida and forgive me for not inviting you to our wedding. I don't know what happened – must have had a brain freeze.

Ulf 'U-G' Göransson: thank you for pointing me in the right direction.

Bertil and Ingrid Jonsson: you both know how much you mean to me.

Kenth and Eva Björkland: thanks for looking after me and putting food in my stomach.

I also want to thank my new friends: Per Björkebaum, Mattias Jaktlund, Andreas Lundqvist, John Nolebring, Gabriel Wennstig and, not least, Patrick Rosenberg – you were the one who got me writing.

Offside Press: without you there wouldn't have been a book. You are brave and that's why you are the best.

Last but least, I want to thank Mogwai, Low and Sigur Rós: without you I would never have stuck to the task.

Also from Bloomsbury:

Running Up That Hill

Outrunning the Demons

Eat & Run

Mindful Running